# THE SHOOTING SCRIPT®

# SLUMDOG MILLIONAIRE

SCREENPLAY BY SIMON BEAUFOY

BASED ON THE NOVEL *Q & A* BY VIKAS SWARUP

FOREWORD BY SIMON BEAUFOY

INTRODUCTION BY DANNY BOYLE

NHB Shooting Scripts
NICK HERN BOOKS • LONDON
www.nickhernbooks.co.uk

This book first published in Great Britain in 2008 as an original paperback
by Nick Hern Books Ltd, The Glasshouse, 49A Goldhawk Road, London W12 8QP,
by arrangement with Newmarket Press, New York.

A CIP catalogue record of this book is available from the British Library.

ISBN 978-1-84842-040-3

THE NHB SHOOTING SCRIPT SERIES

*The Actors*
*Adaptation*
*A Beautiful Mind*
*Big Fish*
*Capote*
*Cinderella Man*
*Erin Brockovich*
*Eternal Sunshine of the Spotless Mind*
*The Good Shepherd*
*Gosford Park*
*I Went Down*
*The Ice Storm*
*In Good Company*
*Margot at the Wedding*
*Saltwater*
*The Shawshank Redemption*
*The Squid and the Whale*
*The Truman Show*
*United 93*

For information on forthcoming titles, please contact the publisher:
Nick Hern Books, The Glasshouse, 49A Goldhawk Road, London W12 8QP
e-mail: info@nickhernbooks.demon.co.uk

# CONTENTS

# FOREWORD

## BY SIMON BEAUFOY

I first visited India over twenty years ago. I was eighteen, alone and rather frightened by this vast land. But among the strangeness lay a comforting familiarity. Connaught Place could be Bath on a very sunny day, Victoria Terminus a grander and noisier St. Pancras; everywhere people spoke to me in English, knew about London, Lords, Manchester United. Echoes of Britain's rule were distant but ever present.

Then I read Vikas Swarup's extraordinary book *Q & A*. Nothing that I thought I knew about India lay in these pages. Intrigued, I went to Mumbai. No trace of the Raj remained, not even the name Bombay. In its place was a city of gangsters, call centers, mobile phones dangling from every wrist, a Bollywood film crew round every corner, and skyscrapers mushrooming on all sides. Here was a modern city that owed nothing to the past and was charging into the future at breakneck speed. The energy of the place, the sense of fifteen million people furiously on the make, was palpable from the rag pickers on the rubbish dumps to the film stars behind their high walls. Which is why Vikas's idea of an uneducated slum dweller turning up on *Who Wants to Be a Millionaire?* is so utterly beguiling.

As I stepped into a country where the monsoon rain is a weapon, the sun is blistering, and the tea sweet enough to strip the enamel from your teeth, the characteristics of the English writer—nuance, subtext, subtlety—all seemed suddenly inappropriate. For the first time in my career, I found myself experimenting with the grand, the operatic, the unashamedly melodramatic. The mystery that was Bollywood's singing and dancing finally made utter sense to me. In this magnificent country of extremes, why would you not sing, why would you not dance?

How the script then became the film is somebody else's story. It is just for me to say that the end product is more than I ever dreamed it could be. And I had quite ambitious dreams. Writing it was the easy bit. So to Christian and Danny, my lifelong thanks and admiration.

—London, October 30, 2008

# INTRODUCTION

## BY DANNY BOYLE

When I was first sent the screenplay for *Slumdog Millionaire* back in August 2006, I thought, "Oh, no, I don't want to make a film about a quiz show!"

Simon is from Yorkshire and I am from Lancashire. The two counties fought the War of the Roses and produce stubborn, awkward individuals who don't tend to mix easily. Nonetheless, I was a huge admirer of *The Full Monty,* and out of respect I thought I had better take a look at the screenplay.

I read it on a gray London afternoon, and the script was literally vibrating in front of me. By page 10—the scene where the two young brothers are chased through the Juhu slums—I had made up my mind to direct the film. Here was a whole new world—dazzling, brutal, dynamic, and joyful—brought vividly and urgently to life.

If ever there was a case for the role of adapter as creator, this screenplay is it. Simon sweeps through Vikas Swarup's novel, grabbing only what is vital, and shapes a work in its own right. Indebted, of course, to Vikas for the original idea but unfettered by any obligation other than to the life of the characters and the "maximum city" they live in, this is bold, vibrant writing that knows where it's going and makes everything work toward getting there.

This is screenwriting as architecture. Simon knows where he is taking you, and the delight is in discovering how he gets you there. Every scene has a beginning, a middle, and an end: a trigger, a purpose, and a destination. And the story has incredible empathy for its characters, an ability to get under the skin of life in one of the most intense and extreme cities on earth. It is never distanced or judgmental. *Slumdog* is inclusive, generous, and immediate.

The text you are about to read is the exact shooting script that I carried with me through the Juhu slums and Dharavi, at VT station and the Taj Mahal, on the Mahim pipeline, and under the Andhieri flyover. It was my most trusted guide through the making of the film and I followed it obsessively.

Here's the architect at work.

—London, October 2008

**"SLUMDOG MILLIONAIRE"**

BY

Simon Beaufoy

DRAFT DATED 1 NOVEMBER 2007

1     INT. JAVED'S SAFE-HOUSE. BATHROOM. NIGHT.     1

An expensive bathroom suite. Excess of marble and gold taps. Into the bath, a hand is scattering rupee notes. Hundreds and hundreds of notes, worth hundreds of thousands of rupees. The sound of a fist thumping on the bathroom door, furious shouting from the other side.

                    JAVED O/S
          Salim! Salim!


2     INT. STUDIO. BACKSTAGE. DAY.     2

Darkness. Then, glimpses of faces. In the half-light, shadowy figures move with purpose. An implacable voice announces.

                    TALKBACK V/O
          Ten to white-out, nine, eight,
          seven...

                    PREM
          Are you ready?

Silence. A hand shakes a shoulder a little too roughly.

                    PREM (CONT'D)
          I said are you ready?

                    JAMAL
          Yes.


3     INT. JAVED'S SAFE-HOUSE. BATHROOM. NIGHT.     3

The thumping at the door continues. The sound of mumbled Indian prayer. Dull gleam of a pistol. A hand cracks the chamber open. Loads a single bullet into the chamber, snaps the chamber shut.

                    TALKBACK V/O
          ...three, two, one, zero. Cue
          Prem, cue applause...

Suddenly, the door splinters as it is smashed through. A burst of gun-fire and white light as suddenly...

4       INT. STUDIO. NIGHT.       4

...we are back in the studio, the gun-fire morphing into rapturous applause.

> TALKBACK V/O
> Go, Prem.

A wall of light and noise as the two walk on stage. Cheering, music, banks of searing studio lights. On stage, Jamal, an eighteen year-old Indian boy-man stares, petrified. He would surely turn and run but for the iron grip on his shoulder of the smiling host, Prem Kumar.

> PREM
> Welcome to *Who Wants To Be A Millionaire*!

More applause.

> PREM (CONT'D)
> Please give a warm welcome to our first contestant of the night- a local from our very own Mumbai!

Under cover of the wild applause, Prem ushers Jamal towards the guest's chair, leaning in and hissing.

> PREM (CONT'D)
> Smile, dammit.

The lights seem to bore into him but Jamal manages a tentative smile. Out of nowhere, a hand slaps him ferociously across the face. Then again and again. Blood trickles from his mouth.

5       INT. POLICE INTERVIEW ROOM. NIGHT.       5

The studio lights have seamlessly transformed into the harsh bulb of an interrogation light. Jamal is strung from the ceiling by his arms.

> CONSTABLE SRINIVAS
> Your name, bhen chod.

Constable Srinivas's hand pulls back Jamal's head by the hair, forcing him to stare directly into the lights.

> CONSTABLE SRINIVAS (CONT'D)
> Your name!

5        CONTINUED:                                                        5

                              JAMAL
                    Jamal Malik.

And seamlessly we are back....


6       INT. STUDIO. NIGHT.                                                6

...on the set of *Who Wants to be a Millionaire*. Prem
leans back in his chair, a man at home in his
surroundings. Jamal sits opposite, frozen.

                              PREM
                    So, Jamal, tell us a bit about
                    yourself.

Close on Jamal's face. Without warning, it is shoved
under water.


7       INT. BUCKET. NIGHT.                                                7

We look up from the bottom of the bucket at the screaming
face of a drowning man. His head shakes desperately,
pointlessly. Then Jamal's face is dragged up again,
roaring for breath. Close on his eyes.

                              JAMAL V/O
                    I work in a call centre. In Juhu.


8       INT. STUDIO. NIGHT.                                                8

                              PREM
                    A Phone-basher! And what type of
                    call centre would this be?

                              JAMAL
                    XL 5. Mobile phones.

                              PREM
                    Aha! So, you're the man who rings
                    me up every single day of my life
                    with Special Offers, huh?

                              JAMAL
                    No, actually, I'm an assistant.

                              PREM
                    An Assistant Phone-basher?

A raised eye-brow at the audience. Amusement ruffles
through them.

8          CONTINUED:                                                    8

                          PREM (CONT'D)
                And what does an Assistant Phone-
                basher do, exactly?

                          JAMAL
                I- I get tea for people and-

                          PREM
                - a chai-wallah! Why didn't you        *
                say?

Laughter in the audience.

                          PREM (CONT'D)
                So, ladies and gentlemen, Jamal
                Malik from Mumbai, let's play *Who
                Wants To Be A Millionaire*...!


9          OMITTED                                                      9


10         INT. POLICE INTERVIEW ROOM. DAY.                            10

Jamal's body dangles motionless from the ceiling. His
head is bowed and he is moaning to himself. The ceiling
fan thumps round slowly. In the corner, Constable
Srinivas mops his brow and lights a cigarette. Hot work.
The door opens and the Inspector of Police walks in. A
rumpled man in his late forties who has seen pretty much
everything. He eyes Jamal, surprised.

                          INSPECTOR
                Has he confessed, yet?

                          CONSTABLE SRINIVAS
                Apart from his name, I can't get a
                word out of the runt.

                          INSPECTOR
                You've been here all bloody night,
                Srinivas. What have you been
                doing?

Srinivas shrugs.

                          CONSTABLE SRINIVAS
                Tough guy.

                          INSPECTOR
                A little electricity will loosen
                his tongue.

                                                    (CONTINUED)

Constable Srinivas brings a box and a tangle of wires out
of a cupboard and proceeds to put crocodile clips on
Jamal's fingers. The Inspector stares, deep in thought.
Sweat trickles down his face. He wipes it away with a
handkerchief, seems to be talking to himself.

>                    INSPECTOR (CONT'D)
>           Every night I get home, "why can't
>           we have a/c like Bajan Chacha? Why
>           don't you care about your poor
>           family, dying in this heat."
>           Twenty-four years a policeman and
>           I can't afford bloody a/c.

Turns on Jamal.

>                    INSPECTOR (CONT'D)
>           But you. You've got ten million
>           rupees ek dum guaranteed, yaar?
>           And who knows how much further?
>           Fancy the twenty million, do you?

Jamal just stares.

>                    INSPECTOR (CONT'D)
>           I think you probably do.

The Inspector nods absently to Constable Srinivas who
turns a handle. Jamal's body pulsates and jerks. He
screams. His body goes limp again. The Inspector goes
over to Jamal.

>                    INSPECTOR (CONT'D)
>           So. Were you wired up? A mobile or
>           a pager, correct? Some little
>           hidden gadget? No? A coughing
>           accomplice in the audience?
>           Microchip under the skin, huh?

Constable Srinivas hadn't thought of that. Grabs Jamal's
arms and starts squeezing them all over until the
Inspector has had enough.

>                    INSPECTOR (CONT'D)
>           Srinivas! Look, it's hot, my wife
>           is giving me hell, I've got a desk
>           full of murderers, rapists,
>           extortionists, assorted bum-
>           bandits...and you. Why don't you
>           save us both a lot of time? Hmm?

Jamal doesn't answer. The Inspector sighs and sits down.
Looks at his watch, nods at Constable Srinivas again.
Jamal's body jerks with electric current.

When the shudders and screams have subsided, the
Inspector goes over to Jamal's collapsed form. Clicks his
fingers in front of Jamal's face to check for a response.

>                    INSPECTOR OF POLICE
>          He's unconscious, chutiya. What
>          good is that? How many times have
>          I told you-?

>                    CONSTABLE SRINIVAS
>          Sorry, Sir.

An excited Young Police Constable sticks his head around
the door.

>                    YOUNG CONSTABLE
>          He's coming! Sir.

>                    INSPECTOR
>          Aré wa, Srinivas, we'll have
>          Amnesty International in here
>          next, peeing their pants about
>          human rights. Get him down, tidy
>          him up, for God's sake.

Constable Srinivas goes over to Jamal and starts to undo
the crocodile clips.

>                    CONSTABLE SRINIVAS
>          Maybe he did know the answers.

>                    INSPECTOR
>          Have you gone soft, Srinivas?
>          Professors, lawyers, doctors,
>          General Knowledge Wallahs never
>          get beyond sixteen thousand
>          rupees. And he's on ten *million*?
>          What the hell can a slum dog
>          possibly know?

Jamal lifts his head.

>                    JAMAL
>          The answers.

He lifts his head, spits blood out of his mouth and says
again, straight into the Inspector's face.

>                    JAMAL (CONT'D)
>          I know the answers.

Titles. **Slum Dog Millionaire.**

11      EXT. CRICKET GROUND. DAY.                                    11

Bright sunlight filtered through the ever-present Mumbai
dust. A group of children are playing cricket on a tarmac
cricket ground. They are bare-foot, dressed in little
more than rags, wiry-skinny and fast on their feet.
Salim, a nine-year old, polishes the ball on his almost
non-existent shorts, comes in with surprising speed and
bowls. The batsman hooks it high in the air. The bowler
screams at a boy in the outfield.

                         SALIM
              Jamal! Catch it! Catch it!

The seven-year old Jamal stares up at the ball, jinks
around trying to get into position. He pays no heed to
the rest of the children who are scattering fast to the
edges of the tarmac. The ball seems suspended in the blue
sky. Shouts from the other children seem very far away.
He doesn't notice that they are screaming for him to get
out of the way. Jamal adjusts his feet for the perfect
catch. Then out of nowhere, a light aircraft almost takes
his head off as it comes in to land on the tarmac runway.
Jamal is knocked to his feet by the down-draft of the
plane. The ball bounces away. Also flattened, Salim gets
to his feet.

                     SALIM (CONT'D)
              How could you drop that? It was a
              sitter.

Then Salim's face turns to one of alarm.


12      EXT. AIRPORT PERIMETER. DAY.                                 12

At the back of a pack of children, carrying a piece of
wood crudely fashioned into a sword, Jamal is running for
his life, pursued by an ancient but surprisingly nimble
Security Guard from the airport who is screaming abuse
and wielding a long stick. The kids dash across a rubbish
dump and disappear down dozens of tiny lanes that run in
between the shacks of the slum.

                     SECURITY GUARD
              Private-ka land! Private-ka land!
              The planes won't kill you, mader
              chod, I will!

Jamal and Salim- also with a wooden sword- break off,
head down a separate lane. The Guard pursues them.

13    INT. JUHU SLUM. DAY.    13

The lanes in between the corrugated iron shacks are three
feet wide, with an open drain running down the middle.
Many of the precarious upper floors of the shacks have
been built right over the paths, turning them into black
tunnels. Tunnels shot through with slivers of light. If
you didn't live here, you would be lost and frightened in
minutes.

But these children are natives and with the practice of
many years, Jamal and Salim zig-zag down the warren of
lanes.

They dodge past people cooking in the doorways, sleeping,
washing clothes or in the case of Vinod, a naked four
year-old, pissing into the drain. Salim shouts a warning.

> SALIM
> Vinod! Musketeers coming through!

Without breaking step, they both jump expertly over the
stream of piss. Not so the Security Guard who gets it all
over his trousers, but doesn't stop the pursuit.

The two children charge past a shack filled to the roof
with chickens in cages who all start squawking. They
break out into the sunlight of the 'main road' of the
slum lined with shops. It is packed: with people, stalls,
bicycles and cows. All modern India is here, drinking
tea, shouting at each other, selling food, playing carom,
video games. Leaving a trail of shouting and wreckage
behind them, the pair approach a brand new Mercedes
almost blocking the lane. Beside it stands Javed, an
impressive man in a beautiful suit and his two Minders.
Jamal and Salim skid to a stop, put their hands together
in respectful greeting and edge ever so carefully past
the immaculate paintwork of the car.

Still in pursuit, the Security Guard also slides
carefully past the car with deprecating bows and smiles.
On past the chai stall where a crowd has gathered to
watch a hindi film blaring from the tv rigged up
overhead. The irate Security Guard gets tangled up in a
bicycle. Jamal and Salim stop to give him a taunting, hip-
gyrating parody of the dance on the tv before scooting
down another tunnel. They break out into sunlight again.

> WOMAN'S VOICE
> Jamal!

Jamal skids to a halt, bumping into Salim who is already
frozen.

(CONTINUED)

                                JAMAL
                    Shit. Mummy-ji.

                          JAMAL'S MOTHER
                    Don't you move a muscle.

The Security Guard arrives and he too skids to a halt at
the sight of Jamal's mother.

                    JAMAL'S MOTHER (CONT'D)
                    Thank you, Mister Gupta. I will
                    deal with these two.

The Guard puts his hands together in grudging respect as
Jamal's Mother lifts each skinny kid off the floor by
their t-shirt and marches them down the road.


14     INT. SCHOOL. DAY.                                      14

The two renegades are dumped by Jamal's Mother into their
desks as Mister Nandha hands out ancient school books.

                          MISTER NANDHA
                    So, the musketeers return. We are
                    honoured. Salim. Or *Porthos*, isn't
                    it?

He crashes the heavy book down on his head. Salim opens
the book. Jamal glances over and turns the book the right
way round for Salim.

                              SALIM
                    I know!

Mister Nandha hovers over Jamal's head. He winces in
anticipation.

                          MISTER NANDHA
                    And Athos.

The book comes down like thunder. Jamal blinks from the
impact and suddenly we are back....


15     INT. INSPECTOR'S OFFICE. DAY.                          15

... in the Inspector's office. Jamal watches Srinivas
fiddling with the video recorder, trying to get a
picture. Through the pebbled glass, Jamal sees shapes
moving along the corridor.

16      INT. CORRIDOR. POLICE STATION. DAY.                    16

The Commissioner of Police is fawning along beside Prem
as they walk. The Young Constable hurries behind.

                    COMMISSIONER OF POLICE
          It is so kind of you to visit our
          station, Sir. A great honour.

                    PREM
          Not at all, not at all. I hope *you*
          will visit *us,* Commissioner.

Out of his jacket pocket comes a couple of tickets.

                    PREM (CONT'D)
          Bring the family. It's a lot of
          fun.

                    COMMISSIONER OF POLICE
          Oh! A thousand thanks, Sir. Missus
          Janda will be overcome.

He turns to the Young Constable.

                    COMMISSIONER OF POLICE (CONT'D)
          chai, you lazy chutiyé, chai!

The Inspector joins them in the corridor.

                    COMMISSIONER OF POLICE (CONT'D)
          Ah, Inspector! Cracked it?

The Inspector moves his head. Maybe yes, maybe no.

                    INSPECTOR
          Nearly, Sir.

The Commissioner is just able to contain his apoplexy.

                    COMMISSIONER OF POLICE
          Nearly? Nearly? When Prem Kumar
          himself has-

Prem holds up a tolerant hand to the Commissioner who
falls silent. Turns his laser-like charm onto the
Inspector.

                    PREM
          Inspector. How good to meet you.
          Clearly the kid cheated.

(CONTINUED)

>                    INSPECTOR
>           Clearly, Sir.

>                    PREM
>           So, it is just a question of how,
>           no?

>                    INSPECTOR
>           Indeed, Sir. The proof. That is
>           all we need.

>                    PREM
>           We are lucky to have a man of your
>           obvious experience on the case.
>           This kid might run rings around us
>           filmi types, but he won't make
>           fools out of the Mumbai Police
>           Force, I can see that.

Forced laughter from the Commissioner.

>                    PREM (CONT'D)
>           In front of sixty million people.

More laughter. And fear.

>                    PREM (CONT'D)
>           Which is what will happen if we
>           don't get a result, Gentlemen. He
>           goes back on the show to rob us
>           all with the whole of India
>           watching. But. I can rely on you.

Prem walks away down the corridor. Stops and turns,
apparently casual.

>                    PREM (CONT'D)
>           Has he- has he made any
>           allegations?

>                    INSPECTOR
>           Allegations?

>                    PREM
>           He's a cunning one. A convincing
>           liar. Don't be taken in,
>           Inspector, don't be taken in.

Walks off. The Inspector stares after him. Goes back into
his office.

17    INT. INSPECTOR'S OFFICE.           17

Srinivas has finally got the recorder to work. We get snatches of filmi dancing- heroines singing on mountainsides surrounded by implausible numbers of flags-cricket and finally after some shouting by the Inspector, *Who Wants to Be A Millionaire?*.

> INSPECTOR
> So, Mister Malik, the man who
> knows the answers. Talk.

We close in on the tv screen where Prem is smiling his crocodile smile and find ourselves....

18    INT. STUDIO. NIGHT.           18

...as Prem asks the first question.

> PREM
> So, are you ready for your first
> question for one thousand rupees?

> JAMAL
> Yes.

> PREM
> Not bad money to sit in a chair
> and answer a question. Better than
> making the tea, no?

> JAMAL
> No. Yes. No.

> PREM
> No. Yes. No. Apka final answer?

Laughter from the audience. Jamal looks confused. Prem waves it away, switches on his serious face.

> PREM (CONT'D)
> Remember, you have three lifelines
> if you're not sure of your answer-
> Ask the Audience, 50/50 and Phone
> a Friend. So, the question:

The lights go down, the portentous music rolls.

> PREM (CONT'D)
> Who was the star of the 1973 hit
> film Zanjeer. Was it A-

(CONTINUED)

18      CONTINUED:                                   18

Close on Jamal's eyes.

19      INT. SHACK. NIGHT.                       19

A tiny shack. A garland of dirty plastic flowers
surrounds a torn flyer for one of Amitabh Bacchan's
films.

20      EXT. JUHU SLUM. RUBBISH DUMP. NIGHT.         20

Salim is sitting on a chair at the end of a rickety
wooden pier, though it is not water, but a sea of rubbish
and sewage that lies below them. There are dozens of
these piers protruding from the slum onto airport land,
each with a toilet shack perched right at the end.
Another man hurries up the pier and hands Salim a coin.

                    SALIM
          Immediately, sir.

Turns to the toilet door.

                  SALIM (CONT'D)
          Bhai, get out of there. Prakash
          wants a shit.

                  JAMAL O.S.
          Not finished.

                  PRAKASH
          Stop your time-pass. This is
          urgent.

                  JAMAL O.S.
          It's a shy one. Since when was
          there a time limit on a crap?

                  SALIM
          Since there was a customer
          waiting, that's when.

He flashes another placatory smile at Prakash.

                  JAMAL O.S.
            (singing/ grunting)
          Come on out, you beauty, unveil
          yourself, my darling-warling....

                  PRAKASH
          Look, kid, I got a bad stomach.
          It's borderline....

20     CONTINUED:                                 20

A disturbing combination of heaving and snake-charmer noises come from the toilet shack. Finally Prakash can stand it no longer.

                     PRAKASH (CONT'D)
           I'm off to Devi's bog. Give me
           that.

He snatches the coin back from Salim and hurries off. Salim bangs on the toilet door.

                     SALIM
           You just lost me good money, you
           stupid idiot-

Salim stops. In the distance, there is the faint sound of shouting, a crowd coming closer. Then the crowd bursts through the outer shacks of the slum, pour onto the rubbish dump and make for the airfield.

                     MAN
           It's Amitabh! That's his
           helicopter!

                     JAMAL O.S.
        Amitabh? Amitabh Bacchan?

21     INT/EXT. TOILET. NIGHT.                          21

Jamal peers through one of the many cracks in the shack. He sees crowds surging around the pier, charging towards a landing helicopter. Salim shoves the chair under the door handle- effectively locking it- and runs down the pier to join the chase. Jamal pulls up his shorts.

                     JAMAL
           No! Wait! Salim, sala! Salim!

Rattles the locked door. Pulls a torn flyer from his pocket advertising an Amitabh movie.

                     JAMAL (CONT'D)
           Wait! Amitabh....

He looks down the toilet hole at the sewage beneath him, the landing helicopter, the disappearing crowd. A final rattle of the door. There is only one way out. He jumps down the hole, sprawling headlong into a year's worth of human waste, managing to keep the flyer out the mire. He runs for the helicopter.

                     JAMAL (CONT'D)
           Amitabh-ji! Amitabh-ji!

Salim is at the back of the crowd, trying to force a way
through, but the adults shove him back. Not so for Jamal.
The down-draft from the helicopter flicks bits of sewage
from his clothes. Disgusted fans curse him and get out of
his way. Suddenly, the red sea parts and there is nobody
between Jamal and Amitabh Bacchan getting out of the
helicopter.

                    JAMAL (CONT'D)
          Please. Amitabh-ji.

Jamal holds out his flyer. Used to signing autographs,
the movie star barely looks at Jamal. He takes the flyer
and scribbles his autograph on it.

                    JAMAL (CONT'D)
          A thousand thanks, Amitabh-ji.

He hands the flyer back to Jamal as his bodyguards                    *
surround him and hustle him into a car. Jamal chases the
flyer across the tarmac, grabs it. Kisses it.


22        EXT. JUHU SLUM. NIGHT.                                    22

From high up, the rickety tin roof-tops of the slum seem
to stretch to the horizon. There is a distant shout, a
figure waving an arm.

                    MAN
          It's coming!

Then another shout and another, a chain of voices coming
closer. People come out of their doorways with pails and
buckets. The shouts come closer until we see a naked
figure entirely encased in bubbles dancing and singing in
the lane. Jamal is the happiest boy in the slum.

                    JAMAL
               (singing)
          Amitabh, Amitabh, oh Amitabh! I
          have your autograph, oh, holy
          Amitabh!

                    MOTHER
          Here it comes!

Water comes bubbling through a hose and Jamal's mother
hoses down her ecstatic son.

23     EXT. JUHU SLUM. NIGHT.               23

Not far away, Salim wanders to Mister Chi's stall. He glances around to make sure everybody is glued to the hindi film on Mister Chi's tv and surreptitiously slips Mister Chi the signed flyer. Mister Chi takes a look and gives Salim a small wad of rupees. He sticks the money in his pocket, slinks away.

24     EXT. JUHU SLUM. NIGHT.               24

A tear-stained Jamal is furiously trying to batter Salim, but Salim's extra strength and height means that he can keep Jamal at bay with one hand, Jamal's flailing fists punching thin air.

> JAMAL
>
> Sala! Sala!

Salim's laughter only makes Jamal cry harder.

25     INT. INSPECTOR'S OFFICE. NIGHT.         25

Close on the tv screen in the Inspector's office. Prem ponders Jamal's choice. Presses a button on his computer.

> PREM V/O
>
> You chose A- Amitabh Bacchan.
> Guess what? You just won one
> thousand rupees!

Applause on screen. The Inspector looks at Jamal. Jamal shrugs.

> JAMAL
>
> You don't have to be a genius.

> CONSTABLE SRINIVAS
>
> I knew it was Amitabh.

> JAMAL
>
> Like I said.

Constable Srinivas twists Jamal's arm behind his back, evincing a squeal of pain from Jamal.

> JAMAL (CONT'D)
> (squealing)
> He's the most famous man in
> India...!

(CONTINUED)

The Inspector stares at Jamal, turns back to the tv where
Prem is asking the next question.

> PREM O/S
> For four thousand rupees....the
> national emblem of India is a
> picture of three lions. What is
> written underneath? Is it...

26          INT. STUDIO. NIGHT.                                      26

> PREM
> ...A) The truth alone triumphs. B)
> Lies alone triumph. C) Fashion
> alone triumphs. D) Money alone
> triumphs.

Prem shoots a mock puzzled look out to the audience
eliciting giggles from them.

> PREM (CONT'D)
> What do we think, Jamal? The most
> famous phrase in our country's
> history. Maybe you want to phone a
> friend?

Laughter from the audience. The studio lights bear down
on Jamal. a drop of sweat trickles down his forehead.
Prem is loving his discomfort.

> PREM (CONT'D)
> Or Ask the Audience? I have a
> hunch they might just know the
> answer. What do we think?

He gestures expansively at his audience. Oh, they love
him.

> JAMAL
> Yes.

> PREM
> (startled)
> Yes?

> JAMAL
> Ask the audience.

Prem whistles. Raises his eyes at the audience.

> PREM
> Well, you're the contestant,
> Jamal.
> (MORE)

26    CONTINUED:

                          PREM (CONT'D)
                 Put the poor man out of his
                 misery, Ladies and Gentlemen.
                 Press your key-pad now.

The lights dim. Portentous music.

27    INT. INSPECTOR'S OFFICE. DAY.                    27

The Inspector presses pause. Sighs.

                          INSPECTOR
                 So, Jamal. My five-year-old
                 daughter knows the answer to that,
                 but you don't. Strange for a
                 millionaire genius. What happened?
                 Your accomplice nip out for a
                 piss, did he? Or did he just not
                 cough loud enough?

Silence. Constable Srinivas kicks Jamal's chair.

                          CONSTABLE SRINIVAS
                 The Inspector asked you a
                 question.

                          JAMAL
                 How much is bhelpuri at Jeevan's
                 stall on Chowpatty Beach?

                          INSPECTOR
                 What?

                          JAMAL
                 One bhelpuri. How much?

                          CONSTABLE SRINIVAS
                     (can't help himself)
                 Ten rupees.

                          JAMAL
                 Wrong. Fifteen since Divali. Who
                 stole Constable Varma's bicycle
                 outside Dadar Station last
                 Thursday?

                          INSPECTOR
                     (amused)
                 You know who that was?

                          JAMAL
                 Everyone in Juhu knows that. Even
                 five year-olds.

Despite himself, the Inspector laughs. Then leans in.

                                              (CONTINUED)

                              INSPECTOR
                    I'll give you five hundred rupees
                    if you just admit it. You go home,
                    I go home. Everybody happy.

Jamal just stares back.

                          INSPECTOR (CONT'D)
                    No, you want to go back on the
                    programme and win twenty million
                    rupees, don't you?

                              JAMAL
                    Wouldn't you?

28        INT. STUDIO. NIGHT.                                       28

                              PREM
                    The audience has chosen. And,
                    whaddya know? Ninety-nine percent
                    of them think the answer is A).
                    The truth alone triumphs. What do
                    we think, Jamal? A hundred percent
                    would have made me a little more
                    reassured, maybe....

Prem shrugs, makes a show of examining his computer.
Suddenly fixes him with his eyes.

                            PREM (CONT'D)
                    Are you married, Jamal?

                              JAMAL
                    No.

                              PREM
                    Well, don't despair, there's
                    someone out there who thinks our
                    national motto is "Fashion alone
                    triumphs". You two could be very
                    well matched.

Audience laughter.

29        INT. GALLERY. NIGHT.                                      29

The Director is shaking his head.

                              DIRECTOR
                    What the bloody hell is he playing
                    at? He's way off script...

29    CONTINUED:

                         VISION MIXER
               Split up with his girl-friend.

                         DIRECTOR
               Which one?

                         VISION MIXER
               All three, I heard. Nita as well.
               Back with the wife. She's pregnant
               again.

                         DIRECTOR
               Oh, God, that's all we need....

                         VISION MIXER
               Oh, for Sharukh Khan...Stand by
               white out.

30    INT. STUDIO. NIGHT.                                           30

                         PREM
               ...won four thousand rupees!

               Music, lights, applause.

                         PREM (CONT'D)
               One more question before the
               commercial break. What will our
               Call Centre Assistant do next?

               The lights dim. Prem presses his computer.

                         PREM (CONT'D)
               Religion! Interesting. For sixteen
               thousand rupees,
               in depictions of the God Ram, he
               is famously holding what in his
               right hand? Is it A) a flower. B)
               a scimitar. C) a child or D) a bow
               and arrow?

31    EXT. DHOBI. JUHU SLUM. DAY.                                   31

               Right next to the railway lines is a pond of dirty water
               surrounded by shacks in which dozens of women are washing
               clothes. Trains flash past only feet away from them. Down
               the other end of the pond, nine-year old Jamal and Salim
               are splashing noisily with some other children. Jamal's
               mother pauses in her scrubbing, wipes sweat from her
               forehead and gazes up at the leaden sky.

                                                            (CONTINUED)

                         JAMAL AND SALIM'S MOTHER
               It's going to come. Today. I can
               feel it.

The woman next to her nods.

                         WOMAN
               Hope so. My head is exploding.

                         MOTHER
               Yes. We need rain.

Jamal is trying to intercept the ball that Salim and
Krishna are throwing to each other. He's not having much
success. The ball flies overhead again from Salim to
Krishna. Jamal dives for it, misses and goes underwater.
When he comes up for air, he shakes his head, clearing
his ears of water. Then he stops, listens. Shakes his
head again. Definitely something strange. Thunder? Salim
and Krishna are trading catches, unaware that anything
has changed. But Jamal's mother has heard it too. The
faintest sound of shouting, roaring. The wave of noise is
still faint but getting louder. A frozen moment broken
by:

                         MOTHER (CONT'D)
               Run! Jamal, Salim, run!

Everybody stares at her. A train speeds through as she
continues to shout, her words lost beneath the thundering
train.

                         MOTHER (CONT'D)
               Go! Run!

The train goes through, the last carriage flying past
suddenly opening up the sight of a wall of rioting men
wielding clubs, scythes, metal bars. They come screaming
across the railway tracks.

                         SALIM
               Krishna, quick!

Salim holds out his hand to Krishna who is wading with
difficulty through the water.

                         KRISHNA
               No way! You're a bloody Muslim.
               Get away from me!

The rioters leap the tracks and are upon them.

                         KRISHNA (CONT'D)
               They're Muslims! Him and him!

                              MOTHER
                    Go!

Salim and Jamal scramble out and retreat into the lanes.
Salim turns to see his Mother felled by a rioter. She is
surrounded by screaming, chanting men who rain blows down
on her. Jamal runs back and drags Salim down an alley. As
they head down the alley, they get glimpses of burning
houses, fleeing women, a three-year old boy in a doorway,
painted entirely in garish blue. He stares at them. In
his hand, he is carrying a bow and arrow. An eleven-year
old girl dressed only in a pair of pants runs after them.
She has two bleeding red gashes on her back. They turn a
corner and head towards some vans full of police. Jamal
sees Mister Nandha, the school teacher, stops.

                              JAMAL
                    Salim!

Then Mister Nandha starts walking towards him. An oasis
of calm in the chaos. Jamal looks at him with relief.

                         JAMAL (CONT'D)
                    Mister Nandha.

Mister Nandha smiles, walks towards them.

                         MISTER NANDHA
                    Ram nam satya hai, Babri Masjid
                    dhvasth hai.

                              JAMAL
                    Mister Nandha?

                         MISTER NANDHA
                    We have destroyed your mosque.
                    Now, the followers of Ram will
                    drive you dogs out of our city.

From behind his back he produces a knife and runs towards
Jamal, screaming.

                       MISTER NANDHA (CONT'D)
                    Ram has returned to his temple!
                    Ram has returned!

They flee, but Jamal turns, sees the girl, frozen. He
chases back a few steps, hauls her arm. The spell broken,
and they are off.

32    INT. STREET. EVENING.                              32

They reach the safety of the police vans. But inside the
vans, the police are smoking, laughing, playing cards.
Down the street, a man comes whirling out of a doorway,
his hair on fire. He falls into the middle of the street
and is engulfed by rioters. Unperturbed, the police
continue to chat. Salim and Jamal look on, horrified.
Then one of the police men turns, looks at them. Is
interested. Motions to a colleague. Puts out his
cigarette with purpose.

                    JAMAL
          Let's go, bhai.

Salim and Jamal run. The girl follows.


33    EXT. MUMBAI. EVENING.                             33

Salim and Jamal stand on a hill overlooking the city.
Black smoke billows from a large area that is clearly the
Juhu slum. Standing a little way off is the girl.

                    JAMAL
          We should go back.

Silence.

                    JAMAL (CONT'D)
          See if Ama-

Salim shakes his head fiercely, silencing Jamal for a
moment. But only a moment.

                    JAMAL (CONT'D)
          What about Jeevan Chacha?

Salim shakes his head.

                    JAMAL (CONT'D)
          Maybe he-

Salim shakes his head again.

                    SALIM
          - I saw him. He was with them.

                    JAMAL
          But he wouldn't hurt-

                    SALIM
          - he was with them!

                                        (CONTINUED)

33          CONTINUED:                                    33

                           JAMAL
              But-

                           SALIM
              - shut up, Jamal, can't you? Just
              shut up!

Salim turns away and sees the girl. Picks up a rock and
hurls it at her. She dodges, takes a couple of steps back
but makes no real attempt to get away. He finds another
rock and hurls this in her direction too.

                           SALIM (CONT'D)
              Ja!

Then a flash of lightning and thunder rumbles across the
city. Rain begins to come down.

                           JAMAL
              What shall we do?

No answer. Jamal sits down. Salim sits down. At a
distance, the girl sits down. Rain pours down their
faces.

34          INT. BUILDER'S YARD. NIGHT.                    34

Rain as you've never seen. A pile of huge water pipes in
a sprawling builder's yard. Jamal is in one pipe, Salim
above him in another. They are both soaked, shivering,
but have found some plastic sheet to wrap themselves in.
Outside, thirty feet away, stands the girl. Staring.
Salim hisses angrily at the girl.

                           SALIM
              Go away. Ja, ja!

The girl might not even have heard.

                           SALIM (CONT'D)
              She'll have the Security Guard
              onto us, standing there.

                           JAMAL
              Not if we let her in.

                           SALIM
              No.

                           JAMAL
              She could be the third musketeer.

                              SALIM
              I am the head of this family, now.
              And I say no. Piss off, you.

Salim huddles down in the pipe. After a while, Jamal
follows suit.

                         SALIM (CONT'D)
              We don't even know what the third
              musketeer's called.


35        EXT. JUHU SLUM. DAY                                     35

A flash of Jamal's mother being clubbed to the ground.
Her scream.


36        INT. BUILDER'S YARD. LATER.                             36

Jamal wakes with a jolt and a scream half-swallowed in
his mouth. He shuts his eyes tight, trying to force the
image out. His breathing slows and he sees the girl
staring at him. Salim, too, is staring into nothing. The
rain is still falling. The girl goes back to drawing
shapes in the mud with her finger. Jamal climbs out of
the pipe. Looks at Salim for permission or refusal, but
he just continues to stare. So, Jamal walks across to
her. She looks up, wary.

                              JAMAL
              Where's your Mother?

Silence.

                         JAMAL (CONT'D)
              Father?

The girl shakes her head slightly. Jamal takes the
plastic sheet from around his shoulders. Gives it to her.

                         JAMAL (CONT'D)
              I'm Jamal. He's Salim.

                             LATIKA
              Latika.

Jamal goes back to his water pipe, climbs in. Watches her
huddled under the sheet. Sighs, motions for her to join
him. She darts across, jumps into the water pipe and
huddles up next to Jamal.

37      INT. INSPECTOR'S OFFICE. DAY.                          37

Jamal looks at the Inspector.

                    JAMAL
          I wake up every morning wishing I
          didn't know the answer to that
          question? If it wasn't for Ram and
          Allah, I would still have a
          Mother.


38      INT. STUDIO. NIGHT                                     38

                         JAMAL
               D) A bow and arrow.

                         PREM
               Final answer?

                         JAMAL
               Final answer.

Prem stares at him for dramatic effect. Presses his
computer.

                         PREM
               Computer-ji, *D* lock kiya-jaye.

The lights dim, the music swells.

                         PREM (CONT'D)
               Jamal Malik, you answered D? Ram
               is depicted with a bow and arrow
               in his hand. And guess what?
               You've just won sixteen thousand
               rupees! Well done, my friend. Time
               for a commercial break- don't go
               away, now.

Music, applause. Prem switches off his professional
smile. Gets up.

                         PREM (CONT'D)
               Got lucky, huh? I'd take the
               money. You'll never get the next
               one.

                         JAMAL
               You're from the Juhu slum, aren't
               you?

(CONTINUED)

38          CONTINUED:                                          38

                              PREM
                    Hmm? Sure. Know where I live now,
                    kid? Pali Hill. Twelve bedrooms,
                    a/c in every room, two kitchens, a
                    gym and a screening room. Steel
                    balls is what it takes, my friend,
                    steel balls.

The Floor Manager comes over and gives his head-phones
set to Prem. Prem listens.

                              DIRECTOR V/O
                    Prem? Tone it down, for goodness
                    sake. You're making him a laughing
                    stock.

Prem glances up at the gallery with contempt.

                              PREM
                    We're having fun here. They love
                    it...Where the hell do you get
                    them from?

He makes no attempt to hide the conversation from Jamal.

                              DIRECTOR V/O
                    It's supposed to be a quiz show,
                    not a blood sport.

                              FLOOR MANAGER
                    Two minutes.

                              PREM
                    Stop wetting your pants. I'll be a
                    good little boy with the next one.
                    Promise.

He chucks the head-phones back at the Floor Manager.
Glances in the wings. Sees Nita, the make-up woman. Gets
up and goes over.

39        INT. STUDIO. BACKSTAGE. NIGHT.                        39

In the half-light, backstage, Nita dabs his face with
powder.

                              PREM
                    Meet me after the show. Please.

                              NITA
                    No.

                                              (CONTINUED)

> PREM
> Nita, I can explain.

> NITA
> No need. I read it in bloody
> *Stardust*. Didn't even have the
> balls to tell me. "Prem's
> happiness with another baby on the
> way". After everything you said...

> PREM
> Baby, it all happened before I met
> you. I swear to you.

> NITA
> She's got the gestation period of
> an elephant, then.

Prem is about to object. But instead, he laughs.

> PREM
> You see? Amidst all this misery,
> only you can make me laugh.

Scornful but hints of melting.

> NITA
> All this misery...

> PREM
> Her and I- nothing. You have to
> believe me, baby...

Nita turns away. The Floor Manager comes over.

> FLOOR MANAGER
> One minute.

Prem slings himself in a chair.

> PREM
> No. I'm not going on.

> NITA
> Prem...

> PREM
> I can't. Without you, it's all
> pointless.

Clicks his fingers at the Floor Manager.

> PREM (CONT'D)
> You. Tell the Director.

Nita shakes her head at the Floor Manager who by now is
looking very worried.

                    FLOOR MANAGER
          Thirty seconds.

Prem shrugs and folds his arms. Sees her weaken.

                    NITA
          Prem...

                    PREM
          Calypso Bar, private room, just
          you and me?

                    FLOOR MANAGER
          Fifteen.

                    NITA
               (furious)
          Alright.

He grins, jumps up, blows her a kiss, and stalks back on
stage.


40       INT. STUDIO. NIGHT.                                        40

He sits back down, says almost to himself.

                    PREM
          Steel balls.

Turns to Jamal.

                    PREM (CONT'D)
          Okay, Juhu boy, you've had a good
          run. Take your Mother to Khandala
          and eat some chiki.

                    JAMAL
          My Mother's dead.

                    PREM
          Well, your girlfriend then. Even
          better.

                    JAMAL
          I don't have a girl-friend.

                    PREM
          Live wire like you? You surprise
          me.

                          FLOOR MANAGER
            Five, four...

The warm-up man starts the applause.

                          TALKBACK V/O
            ....three, two, one...

Cheering and music. Prem switches on his charm.

                          PREM
            Welcome back to *Who Wants to be a
            Millionaire!* Our contestant, Jamal
            Malik, Call Centre Assistant- from
            Mumbai, is on sixteen thousand
            rupees and has already used one
            lifeline: Ask the Audience. So, my
            friend: are you ready for the next
            question?

                          JAMAL
            Yes.

                          PREM
            Then, let's play.

Portentous music. The lights dim.

                          PREM (CONT'D)
            For sixty-four thousand rupees.
            The British architect Frederick
            Stevens designed which famous
            building in India? Is it: A) The
            Taj Mahal. B) Chhatrapati Shivaji
            Terminus. C) India Gate. D) Howrah
            Bridge. What do you think, Jamal?
            Are you one of those tea-boys with
            a penchant for architecture?


41      INT. CHHATRAPATI SHIVAJI TERMINUS. DAY.              41

Known to everyone as VT station, this monument to
Victorian railway architecture is a dangerous place to be
at rush hour. Even before the train has stopped, men are
jumping from the open doors, or vaulting out of the
windows or from the roof of the train to join the tens of
thousands of Mumbaites streaming to and from work. A
seventeen-year old Jamal squeezes himself out of a train
and shoves through the crowds. He checks the time. The
digital numerals flick to five O'clock. Looks around the
tide of humanity.

42      INT. STUDIO. NIGHT.                              42

                    PREM
          So, what's it to be? Walk away and
          this cheque for sixteen thousand
          rupees is yours. Look, it's even
          got your name on it.

He produces a cheque and waves it at Jamal.

                    JAMAL
          I don't have a bank account.

Laughter from the audience. Prem is momentarily wrong-
footed.

                    JAMAL (CONT'D)
          But I'll take cash.

More laughter, this time with Jamal, rather than at him.
Prem gets up and starts rummaging theatrically through
his jacket pockets and trousers.

                    PREM
          Nope. Looks like the Producer's
          stolen my wallet again-

                    JAMAL
          - I'll play.

Nobody was expecting this. Least of all Prem who has to
rearrange his features into one of surprised delight. He
sits down.

                    PREM
          You'll play?

                    JAMAL
          Why not?

                    PREM
          Well, well, well. We've got a wild
          one, here.

Prem tears up the cheque with theatrical slowness.

                    PREM (CONT'D)
          For sixty-four thousand rupees,
          Ladies and Gentlemen, the question
          once again....

43    INT. CHHATRAPATI SHIVAJI TERMINUS. DAY.    43

The digital clocks show five fifteen. Shoving the
descending river of people out of his way, the eighteen
year-old Jamal is forging a path up steps that cross the
platforms. He pushes to the middle of the footbridge and
leans out on the side railings. He scans the sea of
people, desperately. Then he sees her: the eighteen year-
old Latika, heart-stoppingly beautiful, over the other
side of the station. A world away. She is scanning the
crowd, as wired as he is.

> JAMAL
>
> Latika! Latika!

But though he is screaming her name, his voice is
swallowed by the noise around him. Then he sees two
thuggish-looking men also fighting a way towards her.

> JAMAL (CONT'D)
>
> Latika!

Frightened now, he fights his way down the steps, one
figure against an army of white-robed people.

> JAMAL (CONT'D)
>
> Latika!

> JAMAL V/O
>
> Chhatrapati Shivaji Terminus.

> PREM V/O
>
> Chhatrapati Shivaji Terminus.
> Sure?

> JAMAL V/O
>
> I think so.

> PREM V/O
>
> You *think* so. A brave man, Ladies
> and Gentlemen, a brave man.

44    INT. CHHATRAPATI SHIVAJI TERMINUS. DAY.    44

The commuters have mostly gone. Jamal is pacing the
platform desperately. He stops, stares blankly at the
statue in front of him- a proud, rather pompous figure in
a Victorian frock coat. The plaque reads: Frederick
Stevens.

45      INT. INSPECTOR'S OFFICE. NIGHT.                         45

The Inspector, Srinivas and Jamal are staring at the
video recorder.

>                    JAMAL
>          Yes. Final answer. Chhatrapati
>          Shivaji Terminus.

>                    PREM
>          Is the right answer! Sixty-four
>          thousand rupees to you, Sir!

Applause and music. The Inspector presses pause. Stares
at Jamal.

>                    INSPECTOR
>          And did she come back?

Jamal smiles sadly.

>                    JAMAL
>          I wouldn't be here if she had.

>                    INSPECTOR
>          Pretty was she?

Jamal stares down at his feet.

>                    INSPECTOR (CONT'D)
>          Guess not.

Right in the eyes.

>                    JAMAL
>          The most beautiful woman in the
>          world.

Constable Srinivas snorts. Suddenly, Jamal is out of his
chair and at Srinivas' throat. The combined force of the
Inspector and Srinivas force him roughly back down. He is
again handcuffed to the chair.

>                    INSPECTOR OF POLICE
>          Well, well. The slum dog barks.
>          Money or women. The reason for
>          most mistakes in life. Looks like
>          you got mixed up with both.
>          Srinivas, you need the exercise: a
>          trip to VT Station to check on the
>          statue. And lock your bloody bike
>          up.

                                              (CONTINUED)

45          CONTINUED:                                          45


          Constable Srinivas swears under his breath but bumbles
          out.

                              INSPECTOR
                    That's the chutiyé out the way.
                    Now, man to man. How did you know
                    all the answers?

                              JAMAL
                    If I knew, I'd tell you.


46          OMITTED                                             46


47          OMITTED                                             47


48          INT. STUDIO. NIGHT.                                 48

                              PREM
                    Now we're into the serious money.
                    For two hundred and fifty thousand
                    rupees, ladies and gentlemen, a
                    quarter of a million rupees...the
                    song Chalo Ri Murali was written
                    by which famous Indian poet. Was
                    it A) Surdas. B) Tulsidas. C) Mira
                    Bai. D) Kabir. Remember you still
                    have two lifelines- fifty-fifty
                    and Phone A Friend. Tempted to use
                    one?

                              JAMAL
                    No.

                              PREM
                    No?

                              JAMAL
                    I know this one.

                              PREM
                    Oh. I see. An expert on the poets,
                    huh?

          The lights dim, the music swells and Prem presses his
          computer.


49          EXT. MUMBAI STREET. NIGHT.                          49

          Jamal is studying a piece of paper and reading out
          numbers from it.

                                                        (CONTINUED)

There is something not quite right about Jamal- perhaps
the fact that there are two feet by his ears. Salim is
standing on his shoulders and spraying the numbers on a
wall with an aerosol and a certain lack of confidence.

                            JAMAL
               Four, nine, zero, nine- the one
               with the stick going down, Salim-
               six- stick going up-

Latika's head appears from around the corner.

                            LATIKA
                    (whispered)
        Oi!

But they don't hear. Then she is running for her life
past the pair of them.

                            JAMAL
               Six, one, shit, let's go-

Salim collapses off Jamal's shoulders and all three run
off down an alley past a dozen of the gang's sprayed-on
adverts all reading: "Beanbags- 989 4909661".  A fat
Security Guard with a long stick huffs round the corner.
Chases them up an alley. Nowhere to go except through an
imposing gate that clearly leads to a private house.

                      SECURITY GUARD
               Got you now, little shits.

50        EXT. GARDEN. NIGHT.                                    50

They charge across the lawn, down one side of the house
where all the washing is hanging. The Guard gets caught
up in drying sheets, towels. He fights his way through to
see Salim, Latika and Jamal leaping over the wall to
safety. But Jamal turns, jumps back and grabs a girl's
dress from the line.

                      SECURITY GUARD
               Aha! Little thief!

The Security Guard lands a couple of blows on Jamal's
back as he dodges around him and back across the lawn,
dress in hand. The Security Guard gives up.

                      SECURITY GUARD (CONT'D)
        Pervert!

51        INT. ALLEY. NIGHT.                                    51

Jamal is examining the bruises on his legs.                     *

                         SALIM
            Useless bloody look-out. What good
            is she, huh?

                         LATIKA
                      (infuriated)
            I tried to warn you.

                         JAMAL
            It's okay, Salim.

Latika slips on the dress. Spins. Both of them look up.
Stare. She pulls her hair back, smiles, is transformed
into a beautiful girl.


52        EXT. GORAI BEACH DUMPING GROUND. DAY.                 52

Blazing sun. Diggers and trucks are shifting mounds of
rubble on a rubbish dump that seems to stretch for ever.
Oblivious to the dust kicked up by the trucks,  Latika is
picking up old plastic bags, examining each one and
putting the less worn in a big sack. The dress is
recognisable but dusty and torn. She stoops to dig
another bag out of the dirt, but stops and stares.
Shimmering in the heat, a rickety pick-up truck comes
through the rubbish dump gates. Toots at the Guard who
waves, pulls up in the dump. "Hope Orphanage is written
on the side of the van. A man gets out. Looks around.


53        INT. 'TENT'. DAY.                                     53

Under sheets of plastic propped up on sticks, Jamal and
Salim are sleeping out the hottest part of the day. Jamal
wakes to see a figure standing over him- a silhouette
with a halo of sun behind him. Out of his bag, the man
produces a bottle of *Thumbs Up*. He uncaps it with an
alluring hiss. It is almost an advert for thirst-
quenching affluence. Almost instinctively, Salim and
Jamal stir.

                         MAN
            Hello.

He hands the bottle to Salim, gets another from his bag
and waves it questioningly at Jamal.


                                              (CONTINUED)

53          CONTINUED:                                              53

                         MAN (CONT'D)
                Hot, huh? My name is Maman.


54       EXT. ORPHANAGE. EVENING.                               54

         The hills on the edge of Bombay. Greenery and space, for
         the first time in the film. The pick-up truck pulls up
         outside a building with Jamal, Salim and Latika  sitting
         on a bench in the back. Maman gets out. Drops the gate on
         the back of the pick-up.

                            MAMAN
                Anyone hungry? Come on in.


55       INT. ORPHANAGE COURTYARD. EVENING.                     55

         Twenty children are eating at long benches in a
         ramshackle courtyard. Maman, ushers Jamal, Salim and
         Latika in and sits them down at one of the benches. He
         waves a hand and a giant man, Punnoose, comes over with a
         big bowl of food. The three tear into it. Cleaning every
         last morsel of rice from his plate, Jamal looks up and
         notices a table peopled entirely with blind or crippled
         children. Some of the legless are eating on the floor
         next to the table. Jamal leans over to Salim.

                            JAMAL
                He must be a very good man to look
                after these people.

                            SALIM
                       (glancing at them)
                A saint.

         Arvind, a boy smaller than either Jamal or Salim
         overhears.

                            ARVIND
                We're not allowed to talk to them.

                            LATIKA
                Why not?

         Arvind shrugs. Latika licks her plate, glances at Maman
         who is looking right at them.

                         LATIKA (CONT'D)
                Well, if there are seconds, Maman
                is definitely a Saint.

55      CONTINUED:

As if telepathic, Maman signals to Punnoose and he brings
a large bowl of rice and dhal over to them. Latika looks
at Jamal and Salim. They burst out laughing.

                        LATIKA (CONT'D)
           I tell you, Lord Siva is with us.

56      INT. ORPHANAGE. EVENING.                                 56

Salim, Latika, Jamal and a group of children are standing
in a line singing a doha- ancient lyrics set to music.
Maman is leading the singing, walking up and down the
line listening to each one individually. He stops at one
small boy, Arvind, and listens. Nods his head, pleased,
and continues down the line until he stops in front of
Jamal. Holds up his hand.

                        MAMAN
           Stop! You. Again.

Jamal starts singing again. He has the sweetest of
voices. Untrained but pure. Maman smiles, ruffles Jamal's
hair, impressed.

                        MAMAN (CONT'D)
           Everyone.

They all join in. Maman continues down the line. He stops
at Salim whose octave-slipping singing is lusty and
appallingly out of tune. Maman winces and moves on.
Standing next to Salim, Latika giggles. Immediately,
Salim is on her. Before a fight breaks out, Punnoose
pulls Salim off Latika and hurls him across the room.
Salim gets up and charges at Punnoose. For a second,
Punnoose is back-footed, but then pins Salim's arms to
his side. Maman laughs. Approaches Salim.

                        MAMAN (CONT'D)
              You sing like one, and you fight
              like one. I think you've found
              your dog, Punnoose.

57      EXT. CENTRAL MUMBAI TRAFFIC. DAY.                        57

A group of children are sitting in the jumble of concrete
under a motorway flyover. Cars surround them, bumper to
bumper. Latika and Jamal are playing an improvised
hopscotch on concrete slabs. They are giggling, bumping
into each other, tickling, laughing. Salim and Punnoose
are sitting together, smoking. Salim is staring hard at
Jamal and Latika until Punnoose grunts, a sign for Salim
to clap his hands.

                                             (CONTINUED)

>                    SALIM
>          Okay, let's go, let's go! It's not
>          a bloody holiday!

The children get to their feet. Latika sighs, puts a
patch over her eye and grabs a pair of crutches.
Suddenly, the lame beggar. Salim goes over to one of the
girls, who is carrying a sleeping baby. Puts out his
hand.

>                    SALIM (CONT'D)
>          Give me that.

The girl shakes her head. Salim grabs her by the hair in
one hand and takes the baby with the other. He shoves her
to the ground. The other children stare.

>                    JAMAL
>          Hey, Salim!

He challenges Jamal.

>                    SALIM
>          What, choté bhai? You got a
>          problem?

He laughs and walks over to Latika.

>                    SALIM (CONT'D)
>          Here. For you.

>                    LATIKA
>          I don't want it.

>                    SALIM
>          You'll earn double. I'm doing  you
>          a favour, Latika.

>                    JAMAL
>          She doesn't want it.

>                    SALIM
>          Chup, Jamal.

Latika turns away and begins to walk towards the cars.

>                    SALIM (CONT'D)
>          I'll drop it.

He holds the baby up. Latika grabs the baby with a cry
just as Salim releases it from his hands. Salim pinches
the baby.

                                                                                        (CONTINUED)

> SALIM (CONT'D)
> Triple if it's crying.

Latika snatches it away. Salim laughs, goes back to
sitting with Punnoose. The children scatter to the cars
trapped at the lights, tapping plaintively on the windows
and making the universal begging gesture.


58      INT. ORPHANAGE. COURTYARD. DAY.                   58     *

A fiercely hot afternoon. A few children playing lazily     *
in the courtyard, others asleep on mattresses in the        *
shade. Surrounded by beer bottles, Punnoose is slumped      *
asleep by the kitchen door. Salim too is asleep on a        *
mattress.                                                    *


58A     INT. ORPHANAGE KITCHEN. DAY.                     58A    *

Latika edges past the sleeping Punnoose, avoids the cook     *
sleeping under the table and goes to a shelf laden with
vegetables. She pulls down a bunch of chillies still on
the vine, strips a few off, crushes them in her hands and    *
nips back out again.                                          *


58B     INT. ORPHANAGE. COURTYARD. DAY.                  58B    *

Most of the children in the courtyard are transfixed now     *
as Latika carefully pulls up Salim's lunghi. She pours       *
the chillies in. Mild irritation crosses Salim's sleeping    *
face for a second. He shifts vaguely. Then suddenly, he      *
is bolt upright and screaming. He charges around the         *
courtyard clutching his genitals in agony.                   *

> SALIM
> Madher chod, madher chod...! Help!

He grabs Punnoose for help.                                  *

> PUNNOOSE
> What the hell...?

Runs into the shower.                                        *


59      OMITTED                                           59     *

60      INT. ORPHANAGE. SHOWERS. DAY.                    60    *

Two dozen children are screaming with laughter as Salim     *
stands under the make-shift shower directing the water
down his pants to his burning genitals, his face a
picture of agony. Even Punnoose finds it funny. Latika     *
wipes crushed chillies from her hands. Salim points at     *
her.                                                        *

                    SALIM
          You're dead, sali.                               *

She smiles and walks past Jamal with a shrug.

                    JAMAL V/O
          They taught me every song in the
          history of Indian music.

                    INSPECTOR V/O
          And why would they do that, I
          wonder?


61      INT. SHACK. NIGHT.                               61

In a shack, Arvind is singing one of Surdas' bhajans in
front of Maman and an old man who by his ragged
appearance must be a villager. Punnoose and Salim sit
behind Arvind.

                    MAMAN
          Very good, very good. I am
          pleased, Arvind. He is ready.

                    ARVIND
          Ready?

Maman nods to Punnoose. Before Arvind can turn round,
Punnoose has covered his mouth with a cloth and after the
briefest of struggles, Arvind's body goes limp. The
villager puts an old tin box on the table. Taking the lid
from the tin, he brings out a cloth and unwraps it.
Inside is a spoon. He checks the edge with his thumb.
Sharp. Douses it with a clear liquid from a bottle and
passes it over a candle flame. The spoon whooshes with a
high flame for a moment. The villager wipes it with the
cloth nods to Punnoose.

                    PUNNOOSE
          Salim!

Utterly bemused, Salim nevertheless helps Punnoose lay
Arvind on the table.

                                          (CONTINUED)

The villager takes hold of Arvind's eyelid and pulls it open. He brings the spoon close. Suddenly, Salim is being sick in the corner of the shack. By the time he has turned back, the villager is wiping the spoon on a blood-soaked rag.

>                     MAMAN
>           Okay. Take him out the back.

Punnoose picks up Arvind and carries him out.

>                     MAMAN (CONT'D)
>           Now the other one. Salim, go get
>           Jamal.

A frozen moment.

>                     SALIM
>           What?

>                     MAMAN
>           Gunfighter Number One, isn't that
>           right, Salim? The money, the
>           women, the cars...you want them
>           bad, huh? And why not?

Maman gets out of his chair. Approaches Salim.

>                     MAMAN (CONT'D)
>           The time has come to choose, yaar.
>           The life of a slum dog or the life
>           of a man. A real man. A
>           gunfighter, Salim.

Maman holds Salim's head in his hands.

>                     MAMAN (CONT'D)
>           Your destiny is in your hands,
>           bhai. You can be me. Or nobody.
>           Understand?

>                     SALIM
>           Yes, Maman.

Maman nods.

>                     MAMAN
>           So, brother, go get Jamal.

Salim is frozen for another few seconds, then turns and walks out of the door. Punnoose appears at the door. Maman nods to him and he slips off after Salim.

62    INT. DORMITORY, ORPHANAGE. NIGHT.    62

All the children are asleep apart from Jamal who is crouched underneath a couple of wash-basins. He is talking through a plate-sized hole in the crumbling masonry. Latika's eyes can be seen.

> JAMAL
> ...weddings, government things, big parties. If Maman says my voice is ready. Big money.

> LATIKA
> Enough for a room?

> JAMAL
> Easily. Maybe an apartment.

> LATIKA
> Really?

> JAMAL
> That's what Arvind said. On Harbour Road. You, me and Salim. The three musketeers.

> LATIKA
> Harbour Road! We can have ice cream from Babanji's.

> JAMAL
> Every day if we want.

Salim appears at the door. Nods his head at Jamal.

> JAMAL (CONT'D)
> It's my turn.

> LATIKA
> Good luck, Jamal.

Latika's hand comes through the gap. Jamal takes it for a moment. Salim hisses at Jamal. He lets go of the hand and heads out.

63    EXT. PATH. NIGHT.    63

Salim and Jamal walk along the path, Jamal humming happily. Salim checks behind him, sees Punnoose following.

(CONTINUED)

                            JAMAL
                So, this is it, hey, bhai? The
                good life, here we come....

                            SALIM
                      (conversationally)
                Athos.

Jamal is suddenly alert. Slows

                            JAMAL
                Porthos?

Salim nods. Big smile. Puts a hand on Jamal's shoulder.

                            SALIM
                When I say.

64      INT. SHACK. NIGHT.                              64

Salim guides Jamal into the shack where Maman and the
Villager are waiting. Maman smiles. Punnoose slips in
behind Salim.

                            MAMAN
                Jamal, hello. You have done well.
                It's time for you to- turn
                professional.

                            JAMAL
                Really?

                            MAMAN
                Sing me a song, yaar. How about
                Chalo Ri Murali, huh? My
                favourite.

Jamal opens his mouth, then closes it again. Holds out
his hand.

                            JAMAL
                Fifty rupees.

                            MAMAN
                What?

                            JAMAL
                      (shrugs)
                I've turned professional. What can
                I do?

Maman laughs.

(CONTINUED)

64          CONTINUED:                                                    64

                              MAMAN
                    Sala...!

He throws some notes at him.


65          EXT. SHACK. NIGHT.                                            65

            Outside, a giggle. Latika is peering through a gap in the
            wall.


66          INT. SHACK. NIGHT.                                           66

            Jamal begins to sing. Maman waits a while, then nods to
            Punnoose. Behind Jamal, Punnoose hands Salim the bottle
            of chloroform and the rag. Salim approaches the back of
            Jamal. Salim waits until he has finished the song. Raises
            his hand with the rag in it. Maman smiles, nods. Salim
            flings the contents of the bottle in Punnoose's face.
            Punnoose screams and stumbles back clutching his eyes,
            knocking over the table.

                              SALIM
                    Go!

            Salim and Jamal scramble for the door. The knocked-over
            candle catches the spilled chloroform and a curtain which
            whooshes up in flame.

                              LATIKA
                    Jamal!

                              JAMAL
                    Run!


66A         EXT. SHACK. NIGHT.                                           66A

            They charge past the prone Arvind- a flash of bloodied
            bandages covering his eyes.


67          EXT. HILLSIDE. NIGHT.                                        67

            Heavy, desperate breathing. Feet stumble on roots. Fall
            into holes. The three children are running. Branches
            smack into their faces. But they are so scared, nothing
            will stop them. Behind them, torches scour the
            undergrowth. Men shouting. They break out of the woods
            and are confronted with a train goods yard.

68          EXT. GOODS YARD. NIGHT.                          68

They run over the tracks, between the trains, but the
shouts are getting louder, the torches closer. A diesel
engine is moving out of the station. Jamal, Latika and
Salim sprint for the Guard's Van at the very back of the
moving train. Punnoose is closest to them. Salim is
fastest and first to jump the train. He holds out his
hand. Jamal grabs it and is hauled in. Jamal holds his
hand out to Latika.

                    JAMAL
          Come on! Faster!

She reaches out to him. Their hands almost touch.

                    JAMAL (CONT'D)
          Take it! Take it! I can't reach...

Salim barges Jamal out of the way. Jamal stumbles back as
Salim reaches his hand out to Latika, so he doesn't see
Latika's hand grasp Salim's, nor see their eyes lock onto
each other, nor see Salim very deliberately let go of her
hand. Latika stumbles.

                    LATIKA
          Jamal!

Jamal scrambles to the rail. The train gains more speed.
Jamal climbs on to the top rung, makes to jump, but Salim
flings him backward. Jamal tries to scramble to his feet
again, but Salim restrains him.

                    JAMAL
          Got to go back. We've got to go
          back.

                    SALIM
          He'll kill us if we go back.
          Jamal! He was going to take your
          eyes out- with a bloody spoon!

The train is speeding along. Jamal breaks free and stares
back at Latika.

                    SALIM (CONT'D)
          She'll be alright. She always is.

Latika stumbles again and stops running. They watch as
Punnoose catches up with her and stops running. He
smashes Latika to the ground.

69          INT. STUDIO. NIGHT.                                    69

                         PREM
             The question was, for two hundred
             and fifty thousand rupees: who
             wrote the famous song Chalo Ri
             Murali. I should warn you, Jamal:
             from this question on, if you get
             the answer wrong you lose
             everything. So. Are you sure? The
             life-lines are there....

                         JAMAL
             Surdas.


                         PREM
             Surdas. Apka final jawab?

                         JAMAL
             Yes.

                         PREM
             Computer-ji, A lock kiya-jaye.

The lights dim, the music swells. Prem presses a button
on his computer: looks him straight in the eyes for an
age.

                         PREM (CONT'D)
                    (simply)
             Guess what? You're right.

Applause, music, lights.

70          INT. INSPECTOR'S OFFICE. DAY.                          70

The Inspector is eying Jamal, weighing it all up.

                         JAMAL
                    (shrugging)
             Blind singers earn double. You
             know that.

                         INSPECTOR
             And what happened to the girl?
             They blinded her too?

                         JAMAL
                    (shakes his head)
             They had other plans.
                    (MORE)

                                                      (CONTINUED)

70      CONTINUED:                                            70

                              JAMAL (CONT'D)
                    Though it took me a long, long
                    time to find out.


71      EXT. TRAIN. MORNING.                                  71

        Salim and Jamal are sitting on top of the train. Jamal is
        staring blankly down the track.

                              SALIM
                    Aré, Jamal...

        Salim puts an arm around Jamal's shoulder. Jamal wipes
        the tears from his eyes, shakes his head furiously.


        Salim gets up. Holds out his hand.

                              SALIM (CONT'D)
                    Come.

                              JAMAL
                    Where you going?

                              SALIM
                    First class, bhai. Where else?


72      INT/ EXT. FIRST CLASS CARRIAGE. MORNING.              72

        The ancient train is huffing slowly up an incline. A
        middle class Indian couple with their three children are
        sitting at a table, their breakfast spread before them.
        Into this domestic scene, unseen by them comes Jamal.
        Upside down and still outside the train, he is clearly
        being dangled by his ankles from the train roof. He gives
        a few, silent directional signs to Salim who manoeuvres
        him across, dips his hand into the open window, snatches
        a chapatti and signals franticly to be hoisted up. The
        family continue to eat, unperturbed.

        Then Jamal appears again. This time one of the children
        spots him. Despite Jamal giving her a friendly wave, she
        yelps. The father of the group grabs Jamal's hand which
        has just snatched a samosa. There is a tussle, Salim
        holding onto Jamal's legs, the father holding onto
        Jamal's arms and Jamal in the middle, shouting. Salim is
        losing the battle and his footing. He stumbles and the
        pair of them fall from the train, rolling and tumbling
        down an embankment in slow-motion. Interspersed with the
        seemingly endless tumble are images of Jamal and Salim on
        top of different trains-

        - huddled together against the freezing rain...

- surfing the wind at the front of the train...

- admiring the distant Himalaya....

                    JAMAL V/O
          We criss-crossed the country from
          Rajasthan to Calcutta. Every time
          we were thrown off we got back on
          again. This was our home for
          years. A home with wheels and a
          whistle.

The final tumble as they crash onto flat ground.


73      EXT. RAILWAY EMBANKMENT. DAY.                      73

Groggily, Jamal sits up and groans. Somehow- miraculously-    *
in the tumble, he has been transformed into a twelve year-
old. And Salim a strong fourteen year-old. Through the
haze of pain and dust, Jamal sees something glinting in
the distance- something impossibly beautiful.

                    JAMAL
          Salim? Is this heaven?

                    SALIM
          You're not dead, Jamal.

Jamal clears his head. Sees Salim picking himself up from
the ground. But the apparition is still there.

                    JAMAL
          So what's that?

                    SALIM
     Wow.

They stare at the apparition. The unmistakable outline of
the Taj Mahal rises from the horizon, pink in the morning
sun. Nothing could be more beautiful.

                    JAMAL
          Some hotel, huh?


74      EXT. TAJ MAHAL. DAY.                               74

Jamal and Salim wander under the great dome of the Taj
Mahal. Two tiny slum kids dwarfed by this massive
monument to love. It is a moment of genuine wonderment
for them. Then a tour guide bustles nearby, tourists
flowing behind him.

                            GUIDE
                 ...there are five main elements to
                 the Taj. The Darwaza, the main
                 gateway, the Bageecha or garden,
                 the Masjid or mosque, the Naqqar
                 Khana, the rest house and the
                 Rauza or mausoleum. If you would
                 like to follow me, I will show you
                 the ninety-nine names of Allah on
                 Mumtaz's tomb. As before, please
                 remove your shoes.

Jamal follows the Guide and his entourage into the
mausoleum. Salim meanwhile is studying the line of shoes.
Tries a smart pair of women's court shoes, before
slipping a foot into a nice, white sneaker. A smile
crosses his face. His other foot quickly follows and he
saunters away, all mock-innocence.


75     EXT. TAJ MAHAL. DAY                         75

Jamal comes out of the mausoleum into the bright sunlight
and looks around for Salim. No sign of him. Suddenly, a
German couple approach.

                            ADA
                 Please, what time is the next
                 tour?

                          JAMAL
                 Err-

                          PETER
                 - so much waiting around in this
                 damned country.

Jamal notices that he is standing next to a sign
advertising guided tours of the Taj.

                          JAMAL
                 No, I-

                          ADA
                 - we're on a very tight schedule,
                 you see, young man. Have to see
                 the Red Fort this afternoon. Would
                 it be possible to show us around
                 now? Obviously we understand it
                 would cost more for just the two
                 of us...

Peter waves a couple of thousand rupee notes at Jamal.
His eyes widen.

                                                    (CONTINUED)

>                    JAMAL
>           But of course, Madam. Please
>           follow me.

Jamal stalks off. The Germans follow. Jamal stops before
the monument. Points a confident arm at it.

>                    JAMAL (CONT'D)
>           This is....the Taj Mahal.

A terrible pause as Peter and Ada stare at him. Clearly
more is expected. He moves off at a pace.

>                    JAMAL (CONT'D)
>           The Taj Mahal was built by the
>           Emperor Khurram for his wife
>           Mumtaz who was maximum beautiful
>           woman in the whole world. When she
>           died, the Emperor decided to build
>           this five star hotel for everyone
>           who wanted to visit her tomb...but
>           he died in- in fifteen eighty-
>           seven, before any of the rooms
>           were built. Or the lifts. The
>           swimming pool, however, as you can
>           see was completed on schedule in
>           top class fashion.

He waves confidently in the direction of the fountains.

>                    ADA
>           It says nothing of this in the
>           guide book.

>                    JAMAL
>           With respect, Madam, the guide
>           book is written by a bunch of
>           lazy, good-for-nothing, Indian
>           beggars.

>                    ADA
>           Oh.

>                    JAMAL
>           And this, Lady and Gentleman, is
>           burial place of Mumtaz.

>                    ADA
>           How did she die?

>                    JAMAL
>           A road traffic accident.

                         ADA
              Really?

                         JAMAL
              Maximum pile-up.

                         PETER
                    (suspicious)
              I thought she died in child-birth.

                         JAMAL
                    (nodding sagely)
              Exactly, Sir. She was on the way
              to the hospital when it happened.

Jamal moves on. Ada and Peter exchange a glance.

                         ADA
                    (shrugging)
              You've seen the way they drive
              around here...


76     EXT. TAJ MAHAL. DAY.                                    76

Montage of Jamal authoritatively showing tourists around
the Taj Mahal.

                         JAMAL V/O
              It was the best-paid job I've
              ever had.

                         JAMAL
              This is the Princess Diana seat,
              Madam. Allow me.

Jamal shows the tourist a battered postcard of Princess
Diana, staring doe-eyed into the distance with the Taj
behind. The tourist sits. Jamal adjusts her legs so that
they match the postcard. Takes the photo....

                         SALIM O/S
              Tourist police!

...and abandons the woman with a polite bow, charging for
safety as two Police Officers race towards him.

                                              CUT TO:

77          EXT. TAJ MAHAL. DAY.                          77

Jamal stands a Tourist on a wall and positions his hands
to create the optical illusion that he is dangling the
Taj from his fingers. Takes a photo for the Tourist.
Behind the Tourist, Salim and a boy called Shankar pick
up the Tourist's shoes and saunter casually across the
grass.

                                             CUT TO:

78          EXT. ROADSIDE MARKET. AGRA. DAY.             78

By the side of a busy market street Salim stands next to
a row of stolen shoes. Sneakers, court shoes, sandals,
high heels...he is busy bartering with a man over a pair
whilst Jamal tries to shout up business.

                    JAMAL
          Top-class fashion, bottom-class
          prices! Shoes for all! Shoes for
          all!

79          EXT. BOYS CAMP, YAMUNA RIVER. DAY.           79

Hectares of drying clothes by the side of the river.
Spectacular squares of red, saffron, white. Not far away
from the dhobi ghat, there is a makeshift slum-camp where
Salim and a gang of children are sitting, smoking. Jamal
joins them, hands over a wad of rupees to Salim. Salim
counts the cash, hands half to Shankar and slaps Jamal so
hard on the back that he nearly falls over.

                    JAMAL V/O
          And life was good.

80          EXT. SLUM. DAY.                              80

Jamal gets out of a new Mercedes driven by an Indian Man.
A middle-aged American couple also get out. Jamal points
them down a lane which opens out on India's largest dhobi
where hundreds of women are beating clothes on stone
slabs.

                    JAMAL
          This is the biggest dhobi ghat in
          the whole of India, Mister David.
                    (MORE)

                                             (CONTINUED)

                         JAMAL (CONT'D)
                They say that every man in Uttar
                Pradesh is wearing a kurta that
                has been washed here at least one
                time.

                         CLARK
                Is that so? That's amazing. Let's
                get a look at this, Adele.

He gets out his video camera and wanders towards the
dhobi ghat. Behind them a motor rickshaw pulls up. Salim,
Shankar and a couple of the street kids from the Taj leap
out. Within seconds, the Mercedes is up on bricks and the
wheels are being removed. Salim takes a hacksaw to the
Mercedes badge on the bonnet, whilst urging the others
on.

                         SALIM
                Aré, sala! Formula One, Formula
                One! Pit-stop ka speed, Schumacher
                ka ishtyle

The crowds in the lane barely notice as the car is
stripped of all its parts.

                       SALIM (CONT'D)
                Go, go!

A shout from the top of the lane and the boys scatter,
bouncing the four wheels at speed down the lane. Jamal,
the Indian driver and the two Americans return. They stop
in front of the denuded car.

                         CLARK
                Woah. What happened here?

Suddenly the Indian driver is slapping Jamal ferociously
around the head with one of his shoes.

                         DRIVER
                I give you two tight slaps, mader
                chod!

                         JAMAL
                I don't know! I didn't do it, did
                I...? Nothing to do with me...get
                off!

But the beating continues, the driver kicking Jamal down
onto the floor. The two Americans stare, uncertain what
to do.

                         ADELE
Do something, Clark.

(CONTINUED)

                              CLARK
                Well, I- I dunno, I-

Finally Clark intervenes, pulling the driver off Jamal.

                          CLARK (CONT'D)
                Okay, okay, just cool it. You're
                insured, aren't you? Jesus
                Christ...

Jamal sits up. He is bleeding from his nose and mouth.

                          CLARK (CONT'D)
                You okay?

                              JAMAL
                You wanted to see the 'real
                India', Mister David. Here it is.

                              ADELE
                Well, here's a bit of the real
                America, too, son.

Adele pulls out his wallet and rummages for dollars.


81    EXT. YAMUNA RIVER. NIGHT.                            81

A battered Jamal limps along the river bank towards the
Taj. He stops, bathes his swollen face in the river. Then
looks up. Strange lights appear to emanate from the base
of the monument. And then strange sounds.


82    EXT. TAJ MAHAL. NIGHT.                               82

Jamal climbs a crumbling wall and is confronted with an
opera taking place right under the dome. Gluck's Orfeo ed
Euridice. Hundreds of India's smartest professionals are
watching from banked seating on a scaffolding frame.


83    EXT. STANDS. NIGHT.                                  83

Jamal and a couple of street kids slip under the
scaffolding supporting the banked seats. The street kids
are trying to reach the hand-bags of the women above
them.

                              BOY
                          (hissing)
                Oi, Jamal! There's a woman with no
                panties on over here.

Jamal reaches up and easily lifts a wallet from a man's
trouser pocket. On stage, the actors start singing. Jamal
seems to have forgotten the wallet and stares,
mesmerised, at the stage.

> WOMAN
> Why don't you put it back and
> listen to the music?

Jamal starts, makes to run, but the woman who spoke holds
out a cigarette. A Canadian back-packer is sitting,
staring at the singers.

> WOMAN (CONT'D)
> It's called Orfeo. Orpheus and
> Eurydice. Orpheus- that one there-
> is looking for his lover,
> Eurydice. She died, but he can't
> live without her.

She hands him a cigarette. He puts the wallet back. She
smiles at him and they both turn to the stage.

> WOMAN (CONT'D)
> The pain is so bad that he goes to
> the underworld- the place we go
> when we die- to try to get her
> back.

> JAMAL
> You can't do that. Can you?

> WOMAN
> (shrugging)
> You can in opera.

> JAMAL
> Does he find her?

> WOMAN
> Watch and see.

Jamal watches as Orpheus sings one of the most beautiful
pieces of music a human is likely to hear. Tears are
running down Jamal's cheeks.

84     EXT. YAMUNA RIVER. NIGHT.                                      84

Salim, Shankar, Jamal and the Taj Gang are gathered
around a campfire. All of them wear extraordinary foot-
wear of one form or another, from elaborate high heels to
walking boots five sizes too large. A home-made hooka
pipe is being passed around the fire.

(CONTINUED)

The eyes of the children have long since stopped
focussing. Salim is sporting a Mercedes Benz badge on a
chain around his neck. Behind him, Jamal appears, his
face swollen. He takes off his fake Guide's Badge and
throws it in the fire.

                    SALIM
          Woah! What are you- Jamal?

                    JAMAL
          We have to go, Salim.

                    SALIM
          Go? Go where?

                    JAMAL
          Bombay.

                    SALIM
          Don't be stupid. We're making good
          money here.

                    JAMAL
          We should have gone a long time
          ago.

Salim turns to Shankar with sudden understanding.

                    SALIM
          Oh, God. Baby brother's in love.
          With a flat-chested hijra.

                    JAMAL
          Latika was one of us. A musketeer.

                    SALIM
          A musketeer...Grow up, Jamal.
          Look, how was I to know they'd
          beat you up. Here, you can have
          some of the cash. Come on...

                    JAMAL
          I've got cash.

He rips out a wad of dollar bills from his pocket.

                    JAMAL (CONT'D)
          Dollars.

                    SALIM
          How much?

                    JAMAL
          Enough. I'm getting my stuff.

(CONTINUED)

He walks off.

> SALIM
> Wait! Jamal! Ah, shit!

He gets up, kicks the fire in rage and stomps after
Jamal.

85    INT. STUDIO. NIGHT.                         85

Prem leans back in his chair.

> PREM
> So, my friend: ready for another
> question.

> JAMAL
> Yes.

Prem presses his computer. The lights dim again, the
music comes up.

> PREM
> For a straight one million rupees,
> Ladies and Gentlemen...On an
> American One Hundred Dollar Bill
> there is a portrait of which
> American statesman? Is it A),
> George Washington, B) Franklin
> Roosevelt, C) Benjamin Franklin,
> D) Abraham Lincoln?

Silence from Jamal.

> PREM (CONT'D)
> Pay or play, Jamal? All you have
> to do is stop now and you walk
> away with a cool quarter of a
> million rupees. Decide to play,
> get the answer wrong and you walk
> away with absolutely nothing. But,
> get the answer right and you win a
> million rupees. So. You decide.
> Pay or play?

A long pause.

86    INT. GALLERY. NIGHT.           86

>                    DIRECTOR
>          Okay, he hasn't got a clue. This
>          is going to be a walk-away.  Stand
>          by.
>
>                    VISION MIXER
>          No, he's going to play with him,
>          first.

87    INT. STUDIO. NIGHT.           87

>                    PREM
>          Get a lot of hundred dollar bills
>          in your line of work, Jamal?
>
>                    JAMAL
>          The minimum tip for my services.

Laughter from the audience.

>                    PREM
>          Now I know why my cell phone bill
>          is so high...they pay the chai-          *
>          wallah in hundred dollar bills!
>
>                    JAMAL
>          It's C. Benjamin Franklin.

A gasp from the audience. Prem is caught off-guard.

>                    PREM
>          Woah! We haven't locked the
>          computer, man. You're going to
>          play?
>
>                    JAMAL
>          I think I just have. Haven't I?
>
>                    PREM
>          You certainly have. C. Right?
>
>                    JAMAL
>          Right. C.
>
>                    PREM
>          Not confusing your Franklins?
>          Benjamin for Roosevelt?

                              JAMAL
                    I've never heard of Roosevelt
                    Franklin.

                              PREM
                    There's a million rupees at stake
                    and he's never heard of Roosevelt
                    Franklin...I can't bear to look.

He gives this one to the audience who titter on cue.
Jamal looks confused.

                              PREM (CONT'D)
                    No, no. Don't you worry, Jamal.
                    You were asked which statesman is
                    depicted on a hundred dollar bill.
                    You said C. Benjamin Franklin.
                    Ladies and Gentlemen...

He presses the computer, pretends to ruminate for a while
with his finger pressed to his lips.

                              PREM (CONT'D)
                    Jamal Malik- you chose to play not
                    pay. I'm afraid you no longer have
                    two hundred and fifty thousand
                    rupees....

Prem leans over and tears up the cheque. There is a sigh
of disappointment from the audience, a look of confusion
on Jamal's face.

                              PREM (CONT'D)
                    ...you in fact have one million
                    rupees!

Wild applause from the audience. Jamal allows himself a
genuine smile.

87  INT. INSPECTOR'S OFFICE. DAY.                          88

The Inspector pulls out a note from his wallet. Glances
at it.

                              INSPECTOR
                    Who's on the thousand rupee note?

                              JAMAL
                    I don't know.

He waves the note at him.

(CONTINUED)

                              INSPECTOR
                It's Gandhi!

                              JAMAL
                I've heard of him.

The Inspector kicks his chair.

                              INSPECTOR
                Don't get clever or I'll get the
                electricity out again.

                              JAMAL
                They didn't ask me that question.
                I don't know why. Ask them.

The Inspector stares hard at Jamal.

                              INSPECTOR
                Funny, you don't seem that
                interested in money.

Then, Constable Srinivas stomps back into the office,
sweat pouring from him.

                         CONSTABLE SRINIVAS
                Platform Seventeen-

Has to consult his notebook.

                    CONSTABLE SRINIVAS (CONT'D)
                A statue of Frederick Stevens,
                architect and builder of Victoria
                Terminus in -

                         INSPECTOR OF POLICE
                - yes, yes, Srinivas. The hundred
                dollar bill.

89        EXT. BOMBAY. DAY.                                              89

From a thousand feet in the sky, looking down on the
limitless megatropolis of Mumbai. Half-built skyscrapers, slums, factories, roads, trains.

                              JAMAL V/O
                Bombay had turned into Mumbai.

We descend, down until the lines of ants become people.

                         JAMAL V/O (CONT'D)
                The orphanage had gone, the slum
                had gone, the people.... all gone.
                              (MORE)

                                                    (CONTINUED)

89      CONTINUED:                                              89
                          JAMAL V/O (CONT'D)
                  And everywhere was building,
                  building, building.

        Descending even further, we pick out a construction site
        and then Jamal....


90      EXT. CONSTRUCTION SITE. DAY.                            90

        ..who is staring through a wire fence at the construction
        site.

                          JAMAL V/O
                  But I knew she was here. Somewhere
                  she was here.

        He turns away, then something catches his eye. Underneath
        all the scraps of flyers and posters on a broken wall is
        a corner of something that Jamal recognises. He tears
        back a poster. Underneath, faded but recognisable is one
        of their beanbag graffiti advertisements.


91      EXT. SLUM. NIGHT.                                       91

        Jamal asks a group of stall-holders on the slum main
        street. They shrug, aren't interested. The camera pulls
        up and up until Jamal is nothing but a dot wandering the
        maze of lanes, railways and highways, one among endless
        millions of people.

                          JAMAL V/O
                  Evenings, I searched. Days, I
                  worked.


92      EXT. HOTEL. DAY.                                        92

        Jamal wanders up to the rickshaw drivers parked outside
        the hotel. He stops and asks a question. The drivers
        shake their heads. Jamal continues up the steps towards a
        door, exhausted face and grubby clothes walking straight
        towards camera. He goes through the door and
        immediately....


93      INT. HOTEL. FOYER. DAY.                                 93

        ....is, without breaking step in a slightly grubby white
        uniform. He walks across the echoing, marble floor of a
        struggling four-star hotel, goes through double doors....

94      INT. HOTEL CORRIDOR. DAY.          94

...into a corridor that is devoid of carpet, paint-
anything except a phone on the bare wall and a stool. The
phone is ringing. Jamal sits on the stool and answers the
phone.

> JAMAL
> Room service, good afternoon?...
> Yes, sir. Two chicken burgers, two
> fries, one cocoa-cola and one
> mango lassi and a large bottle of
> mineral water...Bisleri or
> Himalayan Spring,
> Sir?...Certainly, Sir. That will
> be with you in fifteen minutes,
> Sir. Thank you. Have a nice day.

He hangs up and goes through another set of doors...

95      INT. HOTEL KITCHENS. DAY.          95

...to a cramped kitchen with definite hygiene problems.
The cooks are playing carom on the table while under it
Salim is dozing.

> JAMAL
> Two chicken burgers, coke, mango
> lassi and a bottle of Bisleri.

Dozily, Salim gets up and takes a look behind one of the
fridges. He chases out a chicken with a desultory kick
and sorts through some empty mineral water bottles until
he finds a Bisleri bottle. Salim fills the bottle of
mineral water from the tap and begins delicately re-
sealing the tamper-proof lid with super-glue. Jamal
collects cutlery and starts laying out a tray.

> JAMAL (CONT'D)
> I'm going to Chowpatti again,
> okay? Want to come?

> SALIM
> For God's sake. You got some
> disease? You force me back to this
> shit-hole, we leave our friends, a
> good life, loads of money- for
> this. Isn't that enough?

> JAMAL
> We came back to find her.

(CONTINUED)

> SALIM
> No, *you* did, Jamal, not me. Me, I
> don't give a shit about her.
> Plenty of pussy in Bombay for
> Salim. Oh, yes, sir! You should
> come down the Cages on Saturday
> night instead of searching for
> your lost love.

> JAMAL
> I'm going to Chowpatti.

> SALIM
> (impersonating Jamal)
> "I'm going to Chowpatti". There
> are nineteen million people in
> this city, Jamal. Forget her.
> She's history.

> JAMAL V/O
> But she wasn't.

96    EXT. BANDRA BANDSTAND. DAY.                              96

Jamal is dodging the traffic at a busy junction. He moves
around the beggars who are working the cars. Then he
hears singing. He looks around, suddenly panicked. It is
a siren song drawing him across the road, not even
noticing that he is narrowly run down by a couple of
cars, to a traffic island underneath a flyover. He turns
a corner and there is the singer, leaning up against one
of the struts of the flyover. Arvind. Older now, just
like Jamal, a fourteen year-old boy. But eye-less. Jamal
freezes. He approaches Arvind and waits until he has
finished singing. Despite his eyeless sockets, Arvind
appears to know somebody is there. He turns and bows low,
putting his hands together.

> ARVIND
> Namaste, Sahib. Any kindness you
> give will be repaid in heaven many
> times.

Jamal gets a couple of notes out of his pocket and puts
them into Arvind's outstretched hand. He feels the notes
with his fingers.

> ARVIND (CONT'D)
> A fifty. And a hundred! Blessings
> upon you, Sahib.

> JAMAL
> How do you know?

                                                  (CONTINUED)

                    ARVIND
          There are many ways of seeing.

Arvind puts his hands together and bows deep again. Then,
Jamal takes his shoe off and gets out a hundred dollar
bill.

                    JAMAL
          Here.

Jamal crouches down and puts the bill into Arvind's hand.
His fingers feel it. He sniffs it.

                    ARVIND
          Dollars. But how many?

                    JAMAL
          One hundred.

                    ARVIND
          Now you are playing with me,
          Sahib.

                    JAMAL
          No. I swear.

                    ARVIND
          What is on it? The pictures. Tell
          me.

                    JAMAL
          A building. With a clock on it.
          Trees behind it.

                    ARVIND
          The other side. Turn it over.

                    JAMAL
          A man- it doesn't say his name. He
          is sort of bald, but has long hair
          on the sides.

                    ARVIND
           (smiling)
          Benjamin Franklin. My God, my God.
          Thank you, Sahib. You were
          generous the first time. But
          this...

He stops. Suspects.

                  ARVIND (CONT'D)
          And without even a song?

                                (CONTINUED)

A long pause. Arvind keeps hold of Jamal's arm.

                    ARVIND (CONT'D)
          So you are rich, now, are you,
          Jamal? I am happy for you.

                    JAMAL
          I am so sorry, Arvind.

                    ARVIND
          You got away. I didn't. That is
          all. No, no tears. Tears mock me
          all the more.

                    JAMAL
          Arvind, I am looking for-

                    ARVIND
          - how's your voice, Jamal?

                    JAMAL
          I don't know. I haven't sung since-
          since then. Arvind, I-

                    ARVIND
          - and your eyes?

                    JAMAL
              (surprised)
          My eyes? My eyes are fine.

                    ARVIND
          Then stay away, chutiyé, and count
          your blessings every morning you
          open them and see the sun rising.
          You owe Maman. He doesn't forget.

                    JAMAL
          I owe Latika.

Arvind shakes his head angrily.

                    JAMAL (CONT'D)
          Please. Is she alive? Arvind, is
          she alive?

                    ARVIND
          Alive? Oh, she's alive alright.
          It's your life, Jamal. Pila
          Street. They call her Cherry, now.

                    JAMAL
          Thank you.

                                        (CONTINUED)

Jamal heads off through the traffic. Arvind shouts after
him.

                         ARVIND
          I will sing at your funeral, yaar.

97      EXT. PILA STREET. NIGHT.                                  97

Dark, crowded streets. Gangs of women stand outside the
doorways or lean out of upstairs windows. They are
garishly-dressed prostitutes varying in age from 13 to
60. Men wander past, eying the possibilities, exchanging
lewd comments with them. Among the hordes on the pavement
are Jamal and Salim. They pass doorway after doorway of
narrow rooms where prostitutes wait for customers. Jamal
and Salim stop at each group of women, Salim taking the
lead, clearly asking them something, as the women either
shrug or offer them something lewd- judging by the
laughter that follows. But one woman in a narrow doorway
points down the street. Jamal has to drag a reluctant
Salim away from the group.

98      INT. BROTHEL. NIGHT.                                      98

They go into one of the tiny houses. Loud Filmi music
comes from upstairs. They are confronted by a woman in
her fifties watching tv. She is less than interested.

                         SALIM
          I'm looking for Cherry.

                         WOMAN
          No, kid. Not available. Plenty of
          others. Take a look.

She indicates curtained cubicles behind him.

                         SALIM
          I'm Latika's brother.

The Woman looks at him properly for the first time.

                         WOMAN
          She's still not on the menu.
          Choose someone else or piss off.

Then, Jamal pulls out some rupee notes.

                         JAMAL
          Just two minutes to talk to her.

She takes the money, counts it.

                                                        (CONTINUED)

98    CONTINUED:                                                98

                        WOMAN
              Two minutes.

She nods upwards. Salim and Jamal head up the dark, tiny
staircase. The Woman picks up the phone on her desk.


99      INT. LANDING. NIGHT.                                    99

On the tiny landing, Salim and Jamal pull back a curtain
to reveal a humping couple. They move on, past more women
lying on their beds or blankly having sex, not in the
least perturbed to be interrupted. They reach the end of
the landing. From the other side of the door comes the
filmi music. Jamal puts his eye to one of the gaps in the
slatted door. Through it he can see glimpses of a girl
dancing to the music. Latika; though not the rag-picker
of before. Now fifteen, she is a beautiful young woman
and dressed in a revealing, turquoise, silk sari.

                        SALIM
              Is it her or not?

He shoves Jamal out of the way and watches.

                        SALIM (CONT'D)
              Shit, she's sexy, man....

Then the music stops, an effeminate man steps into the
limited frame Salim can see and snaps a stick down hard
on Latika's hand.

                        DANCE TEACHER
              Smile! Flow, flow! You *entice* with
              the hands not make chapattis, you
              gawaar. Again.

The man starts the music again and Latika's hands flow
elegantly around her head.

                        DANCE TEACHER (CONT'D)
              Lift your feet, you lump. Stop,
              stop!

The stick is raised to hit her but Jamal opens the door.


100     INT. BROTHEL. NIGHT.                                   100

She can barely believe her eyes.

                        LATIKA
              Jamal?

(CONTINUED)

The Dance Teacher turns.

                    DANCE TEACHER
          What the hell do you want?

He switches off the music.

                    JAMAL
          Come. Quick.

But Latika remains fixed.

                    DANCE TEACHER
          You silly little boys. Get out now
          while you can.

                    JAMAL
          Come with us.

Latika runs to Jamal. But she freezes as she looks at the
doorway. Maman, Punnoose and the Woman from downstairs
stand there. The skin around Punnoose's eye bears the
blisters from the chloroform burn years ago.

                    MAMAN
          Look who we have here, Punnoose.
          Hello again, Jamal. Salim. Never
          forget a face. Especially one that
          I own.

                    PUNNOOSE
          Shall I take them to the marshes?

                    MAMAN
          Whatever you like. Have fun. Just
          make sure that you dispose of them
          properly afterwards. No traces,
          thank you.

He turns to Jamal.

                    MAMAN (CONT'D)
          You really thought you could just
          walk in and take my prize away?
          Have you any idea how much this
          little virgin is worth, bhen chod?

He fingers Latika's hair.

                    MAMAN (CONT'D)
          Get them out of here.

Punnoose and the Muscle walk towards Jamal. Maman turns
to the Dance Teacher as they grab his arms.

                                        (CONTINUED)

>                    MAMAN (CONT'D)
>           Please continue, Master-ji.

The Dance Teacher puts the music back on.

>                    SALIM
>           No.

Suddenly, Salim is holding a pistol.

>                    SALIM (CONT'D)
>           Leave him. Get over there.

Punnoose and the Muscle slowly release Jamal and join
Maman.

>                    MAMAN
>           Let's not be foolish, Salim.
>           Heavy, aren't they?

Salim straightens up his gun arm.

>                    SALIM
>           Money.

>                    MAMAN
>           You can have money. Here.

Maman gets out his wallet and throws all the money in it
on the floor.

>                    MAMAN (CONT'D)
>           Take it. Go. Disappear with your
>           friend and we'll forget all about
>           this. Okay?

Salim collects up the money.

>                    SALIM
>           Maman never forgets. Isn't that
>           right?

>                    MAMAN
>           Oh, Maman can make an exception.

Salim walks over to the music, turns it up. Picks up a
cushion from the bed and walks right up to Maman.

>                    SALIM
>           Can't take that risk, Maman.
>           Sorry.

He wraps the cushion around the gun and pulls the
trigger. Or tries to. Nothing happens.

                                           (CONTINUED)

There is a frozen moment as they watch him fail to shoot.
Everybody watches with surreal interest as Salim fumbles
with the pistol. Eventually he looks up, giggles
stupidly.

                         SALIM (CONT'D)
             Safety catch.

Shrugs apologetically and shoots. Nobody is more
surprised than Maman who crumples onto the floor. Latika
starts desperately gathering up the notes on the floor,
grabs Maman's wallet. Jamal just stands.

                         SALIM (CONT'D)
             Come on.

They run out of the room and down the stairs as Maman
dies on the floor in front of his frozen colleagues.


101     EXT. CHOWPATTY BEACH. DUSK.                        101

Children are splashing in the sea, flying kites, digging
sand, laughing. Salim, Latika and Jamal are crouched on
the shore watching the sun sink into the sea. Latika is
going through Maman's wallet, Salim is fingering the
pistol, admiringly. Jamal is staring out to sea. Each in
their own world, yet sharing swigs from a bottle of
Johnny Walker.

                         LATIKA
             Shit, there's thousands here.

                         SALIM
             We should be celebrating.

                         JAMAL
             You just killed somebody.

                         SALIM
             He was going to kill us.

                         JAMAL
             Where did you get the gun?

                         SALIM
             Bought it. Now, I'm going to have
             to throw this beauty in the sea.

                         LATIKA
             You didn't need to kill him.

                         SALIM
             What? Typical. I save your life
             and you're on at me.
                         (MORE)

                                                  (CONTINUED)

                              SALIM (CONT'D)
                    All you ever do is mess us up.
                    Whenever you're around-

                              JAMAL
                    - shut up, can't you? Just shut
                    up.

Silence.

                              SALIM
                    Why can't you just be happy, huh?

                              JAMAL
                    Happy?

                              SALIM
                    You got what you wanted, didn't
                    you? So, let's celebrate.

                              LATIKA
                    Yeah. Let's celebrate.

She takes a long swig from the bottle.

                              LATIKA (CONT'D)
                       While we can.

She nudges Jamal and holds the bottle out to him. Smiles
at him. He smiles back, shakes the black dog from his
head and takes a long, long drink. Latika and Salim
cheer.

101A    EXT. TULIP STAR. NIGHT.                                 101A

Latika, Salim and Jamal bend back a bit of the wire mesh
fence that protects the deserted hotel. Crawl in.

102     INT. TULIP STAR. LOBBY. NIGHT.                          102

A very wobbly Latika, Salim and Jamal walk up the frozen
escalators of the empty hotel, lit only by security
lights. Kick through the odd pile of rubbish and stacked-
up chairs. Go to the dusty reception desk.

                              JAMAL
                       Service!

                              SALIM
                       Reception!

> JAMAL
> We want a room, boy. Executive
> Class with smoking. Third floor
> with balcony.

> LATIKA
> Sea-facing, yaar.

> SALIM
> Have the bags brought up.

And they scoot off, giggling into the dark.

102A    INT. TULIP STAR. KITCHENS. NIGHT.           102A

Jamal and Latika wander the vast, empty kitchens. Jamal
searches the empty chillers and cabinets. Then, realises
that he is alone.

> JAMAL
> Latika? Salim?

Where are they? Suddenly,

> LATIKA
> Room service!

She comes shooting out of the darkness across the kitchen
floor riding a trolley with Salim pushing her at top
speed. Jamal has to skid out of the way. He grabs another
trolley and glides off in pursuit.

102B    INT. TULIP STAR. CORRIDOR. NIGHT.           102B

The three stand by a mirror and play with their
reflections.

103A    INT. TULIP STAR. HOTEL LOBBY. LATER.        103A

On top of the metal preparation counters, Salim and Jamal
are fencing: Jamal with a fish slice and Salim with a
large spoon.

103    INT. HOTEL ROOM. NIGHT.                  103

An empty, dusty hotel suite. Jamal is on the phone.

103     CONTINUED:                                          103

                         JAMAL
               307 here. I want a bottle of
               Johnny Walker Red Label, beer,
               wine-

                         LATIKA
               - chicken.

                         JAMAL
               Ah! Chicken....

Jamal closes his eyes at the wonderful thought.

                         JAMAL (CONT'D)
               What kind of chicken?

                         LATIKA
                    (also dreaming)
               Tikka Masala. With roti-

                         SALIM
               Naan, chutney, dal-

                         LATIKA
               - aloo gobi, rice-

She stops. Change of mind.

                         LATIKA (CONT'D)
               Pop Tarts!

                         JAMAL
               Hold the line, chutiye.
               Pop Tarts?

                         LATIKA
               On the tv. The commercial.
               Everybody's happy when they have
               Pop Tarts.

                         JAMAL
               Exactly! A *bucket* of Pop Tarts,
               chutiye.

Jamal slams down the phone.


104     INT. HOTEL ROOM. LATER.                            104

Latika is clearly in the shower. Jamal wanders in
carrying an old pair of lunghi. Shouts through the door.

                         JAMAL
               Found some lunghi!

                                              (CONTINUED)

                              LATIKA V/O
                   Stay there. Look away.

The shower stops.

                              JAMAL
                   Atcha, atcha.

                              LATIKA V/O
                   I'll know if you're looking....

                              JAMAL
                   I'm not!

With a towel around her, Latika comes to the doorway
where Jamal is holding out a the lunghi with his eyes
tight shut.

                              JAMAL (CONT'D)
                   Where's Salim?

                              LATIKA
                   Dunno.

She watches this innocent a second with true fondness.

                              LATIKA (CONT'D)
                   You're a sweet boy, Jamal.

She takes the lunghi from his outstretched hand and
disappears into the bathroom, slamming the door with a
giggle.


105    EXT. MUMBAI SLUM STREET. NIGHT.                      105

Salim wanders the crowded streets of a slum. He stops
uncertainly at a doorway where a group of men are
lolling, smoking. Plucks up his courage.

                              SALIM
                   I'm looking for Javed-bhai.

                              MAN
                   Ja, mada chod. He's not looking
                   for you. Ja!

                              SALIM
                   I need to see him.

The group of men stir, irritated now. Salim begins to
back away, then stops. Pulls the gun from behind his
back.

105    CONTINUED:                                                    105

                              SALIM (CONT'D)
                    I killed Maman. I'll kill you too.
                    Easy.

The group are frozen.

                              JAVED
                    *You* killed him?

Javed is standing in the doorway.

                              JAVED (CONT'D)
                    My enemy's enemy is my friend, no?
                    So, come in, friend.

106    INT. HOTEL ROOM. LATER.                                       106

Jamal and Latika lie on the bed, drunk, though still
coherent. Latika is dressed in the Bell-Boy's jacket and
the old lunghi.

                              LATIKA
                    Maman's gang will hunt us. You
                    know that?

                              JAMAL
                    I don't care.

                              LATIKA
                    Me neither.

They burst into stupid laughter. The laughter subsides.

                              JAMAL
                    That dance you were doing. In Pila
                    Street. Show me.

Latika rolls over and switches off the light. Rolls back.
In the half light, her hands begin to move for Jamal, the
elegant, alluring hand movements of the bar-girl dancers.
Jamal stares, mesmerised.

                              LATIKA
                    You came back for me.

                              JAMAL
                    Of course.

                              LATIKA
                    I thought you'd forgotten.

(CONTINUED)

                              JAMAL                                    *
                   I never forgot. Not for one day. I
                   knew I'd find you in the end. It's
                   our destiny.

                              LATIKA
                   Destiny. Yes.

Latika stops her hands. They stare at each other, their
faces inches away from each other. Latika strokes Jamal's
face.

                              LATIKA (CONT'D)
                   Thank you.

And face to face, they slowly fall asleep.


107    INT. HOTEL ROOM. LATER.                              107

                              SALIM
                   Hey.

Jamal opens his eyes. Salim is standing over them,
swaying with alcohol.

                              JAMAL
                   Salim?

He puts his hand out to Latika.

                              SALIM
                   Come.

                              JAMAL
                   No. Salim....Bhai, you've had a
                   lot to drink...

Jamal tries to get up, but Salim's hand is round his
throat and pushes him down on the bed.

                              SALIM
                   I am the elder. And I am the boss.
                   For once, you do as I say.

                              JAMAL
                   No.

Salim pulls Latika to her feet.

                              SALIM
                   I saved your bloody life, didn't
                   I?

107    CONTINUED:                                                   107

                              LATIKA
                    Salim, please-

                              SALIM
                    - chup, sali.

As he turns, pulling a protesting Latika, Jamal leaps on
him. The two brothers go down fighting, but of course it
is Salim who comes up on top. Latika launches herself at
Salim, but he smashes her away, almost delighted that she
has joined in. He drags Jamal to the door, laughing.


108    INT. HOTEL CORRIDOR. NIGHT.                                  108

Salim throws him out into the corridor, slams the door.

                              SALIM
                    *I* am Number One now!

                              JAMAL
                    Salim, no, no....!

                              SALIM
                    Get yourself a room, bhai.

Salim slams the door. Jamal gets up, bangs on the door,
keeps on banging until the door opens and Salim stands
there with the pistol pointing straight at Jamal's head.

                              SALIM (CONT'D)
                    The man with the Colt 45 says
                    chup.

He shoves Jamal hard down the corridor, the gun pointed
at him all the while.

                              JAMAL
                    Salim...

Salim nods towards the fire escape door.

                              SALIM
                    Now go. Or Gunmaster G-9 will
                    shoot you right between the eyes.
                    Boom. Don't think he won't. You
                    have five seconds. One, two,
                    three, four-

Salim cocks the pistol. Jamal screws up his eyes for the
inevitable. But Salim shoves him out with a roar and
slams the door. Jamal bangs on the door.


                                                        (CONTINUED)

108     CONTINUED:                                          108

                        JAMAL O/S
               Salim...

Salim walks slowly back down the corridor as Jamal bangs
and bangs on the door. Down the hall, Salim's door shuts.

109     INT. INSPECTOR'S OFFICE. DAY.                       109

The Inspector is staring hard at Jamal. Srinivas is
desperately trying to get his attention.

                   CONSTABLE SRINIVAS
               Sir, sir!

                        INSPECTOR
                     (eventually)
               Enlighten us Constable.

                   CONSTABLE SRINIVAS
               Accessory to murder, Sir.

The Inspector puts his hands in the air, palms up.
Simple.

                        INSPECTOR
               Only the finest minds in the
               Mumbai Police Force.

Untroubled by irony, Srinivas looks extremely pleased.

                   INSPECTOR (CONT'D)
               Go check the files, Constable.

Srinivas goes out.

                   INSPECTOR (CONT'D)
               You puzzle me, Slumdog. Admitting
               murder to avoid a charge of fraud
               is not exactly clever thinking.
               Now, why would you do that?

Jamal shrugs.

                        JAMAL
               When somebody asks me a question,
               I tell them the answer.

110     EXT. TULIP STAR. MORNING.                           110

At the gate, a Security Guard is sitting in his chair.

                                              (CONTINUED)

110    CONTINUED:                                          110

                              JAMAL
                    Where are they?

The Guard grunts.

                              JAMAL (CONT'D)
                    Where did they go?

A more impatient grunt from the Guard. He stands up,
walks towards Jamal.

                              JAMAL (CONT'D)
                    Please, Sir. Which way?

                              SECURITY GUARD
                    I don't know and I don't care.

The Guard raises his stick and gives him a roar. Jamal
backs away onto the street. The Guard slams the gate
shut. Jamal looks despairingly up and down the street at
the teeming traffic, the crowds.

                              PREM V/O
                    Ready for another question.

                              JAMAL V/O
                    Yes. I'm ready.


112    INT. STUDIO. NIGHT.                                 112

We are back in the Studio.

                              PREM
                    For two and a half million rupees.
                    Ladies and Gentlemen. Cambridge
                    Circus is in which UK City. Is it
                    A) Oxford, B) Leeds, C) Cambridge,
                    D) London.

Jamal smiles.

                              PREM (CONT'D)
                    He's smiling. Why does that worry
                    me?


113    EXT. MUMBAI. DAY.                                   113

Leaden skies. Torrential rain is hammering on the tin
roofs of the slum.

114     INT. SHACK. DAY.                                 114

Eighteen year-old Jamal's eyes open. Now with the
beginnings of a beard and moustache, Jamal wakes in a
tiny shack just big enough for a mattress on the floor.
He pulls on a shirt, lifts the mattress and takes out his
trousers which have been pressing there all night, puts
them over his shoulder, picks up his shoes and goes down
a ladder.

115     INT. SHACK. DAY.                                 115

He descends into a room and two feet of water that is
eddying around the ground floor of the shack. Wades out
of the door into the narrow lane of the slum.

116     EXT. SLUM. DAY.                                  116

Jamal nods hello to a number of neighbours, also bare-
legged, also with their shoes in hand. Together, they
wade to higher ground, put on their trousers and shoes
and trudge up to the main road.

117     INT. CALL CENTRE. NIGHT.                         117

Ultra-modern, glass-windowed office. The words Cultural
Studies are written on the white board. Jamal walks in
with a tray of glasses of chai. He puts a glass down on          *
the young, hip, Teacher's desk and heads out again.

                        TEACHER
            Okay, guys, it's been a big week
            in UK. Kat is back.

He holds up a copy of Radio Times showing Kat from East
Enders smiling at them. A collective groan from the
Trainees.

                        BARDI
            She's already back.

                        TEACHER
            Bardi...Jamal?

                        JAMAL
            Oh. Well. She did come back, then
            she went away when Alfie split up
            with her and now she's back again.
            But it looks as if Alfie still
            fancies Mo after all, so-

                                            (CONTINUED)

117     CONTINUED:                                            117

                        TEACHER
              - thank you, Jamal. Keep up,                        *
              Bardi. The chai-wallah knows more
              than you.

Bardi glares at Jamal. Jamal shrugs apologetically and
goes out.

                        TEACHER (CONT'D)
              Okay, it's been super-duper hot
              for UK this week, so there'll be a
              lot of chat about that- they love
              their weather- and there's the
              festival in Edinburgh- Edinburgh?

He points at a young woman Trainee.

                        NASREEN
              Scotland. Kilts, castles, err,
              haggis? Porridge, the Highlands,
              mountains. Ben- Ben Nevis?

The Teacher points at another Trainee.

                        TRAINEE 2
              Detective Taggart. Whisky, Sean
              Connery!

                        TEACHER
              And lochs. Their word for lakes.
              Good. It's also double bonus time
              for an upgrade to the 'friends and
              family' package this week, so
              remember to push for an upgrade...

                        EVERYONE
              ...Every Call!

Jamal walks out, turns a corner.


118     INT. CALL CENTRE. UK FLOOR. NIGHT.                    118

We are confronted with a room you could swing a Boeing
in. Rows and rows of Operators in tiny booths stretch
into the distance. On the walls are pictures of London,
Tony Blair, red telephone boxes, the Yorkshire Dales, the
Highlands- a snapshot of tourist Britain. Huge posters of
soap stars and celebrities adorn the rest of the walls.
Slogans hang from the ceiling. "When the sun comes up,
you'd better be running", "you snooze, you lose",
"Upgrade for a better, faster life." "Every call is a new
opportunity".

                                              (CONTINUED)

118     CONTINUED:                                        118

Each section of the room has a banner with a British
city's name on it and various mock sign-posts for the
different aisles. A Manager under the banner "Bradford",
is standing over an Operator, listening in on a call. The
Manager leans over and presses a key.

                    MANAGER
          If they want an upgrade, a new
          tariff or we're stealing them from
          the other networks, you take the
          call. Anything else-

He mimes cutting his throat.

                    MANAGER (CONT'D)
          No time-wasters on Team Bradford,
          kid. Leave that to the
          homosexuals on Tunbridge Wells.

Jamal stops by him. The Manager takes a glass of tea from
Jamal.

                    MANAGER (CONT'D)
          Where've you been? Dave on
          Cornmarket's virtually lost his
          voice, there's two on Ilkley Moor
          who've had their hands up for
          hours. Come on, move it!

Jamal hurries down the aisle signposted "Cornmarket, gets
to a male trainee and hands him a tea. Dave glances
around to check nobody's looking and slips off his head-
set.

                    DAVE
          Two minutes, Jamal. I'm on
          "Millionaire" duty.

                    JAMAL
          Rajneesh...

                    DAVE
          It's my turn, Jamal. I've had my
          pee breaks. Please. If he comes
          just keep your head down and
          pretend you're doing an upgrade on
          the-

                    JAMAL
          - 'friends and family'. I know.

Jamal still looks unwilling.

                    JAMAL (CONT'D)
          Two minutes.

                                        (CONTINUED)

118     CONTINUED: (2)                                                    118

Dave heads off towards a Rest and Recreation room, where
a big plasma screen on the wall is showing "Who Wants To
Be A Millionaire."Jamal grabs the jacket from the back of
Dave's chair, puts the head-set on and hunches over the
booth, just another Operative at work. We become aware
that every operator down the Cornmarket aisle- and quite
a few other aisles besides- is staring in the direction
of the Rest and Recreation Room.


119     INT. REST AND RECREATION ROOM. NIGHT.                              119

Dave is watching the screen.

                         PREM
               ...if you want a chance to be a
               contestant on *Who Wants To Be A
               Millionaire*, dial the number now.

Dave dives for the doorway and waves.


120     INT. CALL CENTRE. UK FLOOR. NIGHT.                                 120

Suddenly all the operators are dialling. Almost
simultaneously, twenty or so voices say.

                       OPERATORS
               I'd like to be a contestant on *Who
               Wants to be a Millionaire*.

Most of the Operators- including the man next to Jamal-
suddenly lose their tension.

                        OPERATOR
               Bloody bastard. I *never* get it.

                         JAMAL
               You have to dial when Prem says
               "if". "If you want the chance to
               be a contestant on *Who Wants To Be
               A Millionaire*..." That's when they
               open the lines.

The Operator looks at him. Jamal shrugs.

                    JAMAL (CONT'D)
               That's what Anjum in Technical
               says. He put the system in.

                        OPERATOR
               So why don't you?


                                                            (CONTINUED)

                              WOMAN V/O
                    Hello? Hello? Have I been
                    transferred again, for God's sake?

Jamal freezes with fear. The head-set speaks again with
its broad Scottish accent.

                              WOMAN V/O (CONT'D)
                    Hello? Jesus, God, will somebody
                    talk to me?

                              JAMAL
                    Hello, Mrs...

He stares at the computer.

                              JAMAL (CONT'D)
                    ...Mackintosh from King Gussie.

                              WOMAN V/O
                         (weary)
                    It's Kingussie, love. Pronounced
                    Kinoosie.

                              JAMAL
                    Kinoosie?

                              WOMAN V/O
                    So where are *you* from? Abroad, I
                    bet. China or somewhere. What good
                    is-

                              JAMAL
                    - just down the road from your
                    house, Mrs Mackintosh. Next to the
                    loch.

                              WOMAN V/O
                         (suspicious)
                    Oh aye? Which loch?

Jamal searches desperately around, spots a picture of Big
Ben.

                              JAMAL
                    Loch Big- Loch Ben. Next door to
                    Detective Taggart's flat.

                              WOMAN V/O
                    Loch Ben? Och, no, hen, that's one
                    of the wee ones up in the
                    Highlands. You're all the way up
                    there? But I bet it rains, eh,
                    hen?

(CONTINUED)

                         JAMAL
              Indeed yes, Mrs Mackintosh. I have
              to wade through a metre of water
              every morning.

                         WOMAN V/O
              No!

                         JAMAL
              Yes, yes, Mrs Mackintosh. In my
              kilt.

                         WOMAN V/O
              Och, no, hen.

Jamal puts his feet on the desk.

                         JAMAL
              It's alright once I've had my
              porridge, my haggis and a few
              Scotch whiskies- and the monsoon's
              nearly over, so-

                         WOMAN V/O
              - and what monsoon would that be?
              I'd like to speak to your
              supervisor, son.

                         JAMAL
              I don't think that's a good idea.
              He is a very important man, Mrs
              Mackintosh-

                         WOMAN V/O
              - get me the supervisor on this
              line now-

                         JAMAL
              - and he doesn't like bloody time
              wasters.

Jamal panics, presses the button he saw the Manager press
earlier. The screen goes blank, then reboots itself.
Jamal looks around. Where the hell is Dave? On the
screen, Jamal is faced with the question: "what name do
you require?" He looks around again, and then with one
finger types in the word "Latika". He presses enter.
Hundred upon hundred of Latikas with their surnames and
phone numbers scroll down the page. He erases her name
and enters the name Salim K. Malik. Presses enter.
Fifteen numbers come up. He stares at the numbers for a
long time, then types it into his computer and presses
dial.

                                            (CONTINUED)

# STILLS

All photos by Ishika Mohan

Young Jamal *(Ayush Mahesh Khedekar)* in the toilet shack.

Young Slumdogs Jamal *(Ayush Mahesh Khedekar)*, Latika *(Rubina Ali)*, and Salim *(Azharuddin Mohammed Ismail)* at the dumping ground.

Teenage Jamal *(Tanay Hemant Chheda)* and brother Salim *(Ashutosh Lobo Gajiwala)* discover good business at the Taj Mahal.

Jamal *(Dev Patel)* looks down over his old neighborhood in Mumbai.

Latika *(Freida Pinto)* sets eyes on her love at the train station.

Jamal *(Patel)* and television host Prem *(Anil Kapoor)* on the set for *Who Wants to Be a Millionaire?*

Jamal *(Patel)* focuses on the correct answer while television host Prem *(Kapoor)* waits expectantly.

The *chai-walla* boy Jamal *(Patel)* is interrogated by the police inspector *(Irrfan Khan)*.

Latika *(Pinto)* gets the final lifeline call from Jamal.

Latika *(Pinto)* races to the train station.

Jamal *(Patel)* and Latika *(Pinto)* are finally reunited at the train station.

Their destiny is fulfilled.

Director Danny Boyle sets up a shot with Freida Pinto.

Director Danny Boyle

Screenwriter Simon Beaufoy

                              MAN V/O
          Yeah?

                              JAMAL
          Salim?

                              MAN V/O
          Who wants to know? Do you know
          what bloody time it is?

Clearly not Jamal's brother. Jamal cuts the line. Dials
the next number.

                              SALIM V/O
          Huh. Hello?

Clearly not his Salim. He cuts the line. Dials again.

                              SALIM V/O (CONT'D)
          Hello? Hello? Who is this?

But Jamal can't speak.

                              SALIM V/O (CONT'D)
          Hey. Is someone screwing with me?

Silence.

                              SALIM V/O (CONT'D)
          Who is this?

                              JAMAL
          I am calling from XL 5
          Communications Sir. As a valued
          customer, we are offering you a
          free upgrade with our 'friends and-

Jamal's voice peters out.

                              JAMAL (CONT'D)
          Family.

                              SALIM V/O
          Jamal? Is that you? Brother? Where
          are you, man?...I thought you were
          dead or something...we had to go,
          Jamal. Maman's guys. They were
          searching the hotel...Jamal, say
          something. Please.

There is another long silence.

                              JAMAL
          Hello, Salim.

121     INT. STUDIO. NIGHT.                                    121

                              PREM
                    Ever been to Cambridge?

                              JAMAL
                    No.

                              PREM
                    Ever been to the circus?

                              JAMAL
                    No. And I've never been to UK
                    before. But I'll still have a go.

Gasps and laughter from the audience. Jamal laughs and
shrugs.

                              JAMAL (CONT'D)
                    Why not?

Prem grips his heart theatrically.

                              PREM
                    Can someone call me an ambulance?


122     INT. CALL CENTRE. NIGHT.                               122

A flash of a sign post reading 'Oxford Circus', pointing
down one of the aisles. The banner above that section of
the warehouse reads 'London'.

                                                        CUT TO:


Jamal hurrying down another 'Kings Parade' carrying
glasses of tea. He glances up to see a large banner that
says 'Cambridge'.

                                                        CUT TO:


Jamal comes back up an aisle named 'Broad Street'. An
Operator on the adjacent 'The High' clicks his fingers
for another cup. Jamal hurries under the sign marked
'Oxford'.

                                                        CUT TO:


The signposts of the aisles come faster and faster
'Pembroke Street', 'Trafalgar Square', 'East India Dock'
and finally 'Cambridge Circus'.


                                                    (CONTINUED)

122    CONTINUED:                                             122

                          PREM V/O
                 So, Jamal....


123    INT. STUDIO. NIGHT.                                   123

Jamal is sweating, his face scrunched up in thought.

                          JAMAL
                 I can't remember.

                          PREM
                 You can't remember. Does that mean
                 you did know? Once?

                          JAMAL
                 I don't think it's Oxford.

                          PREM
                 Based on your extensive
                 travelling, right?

                          JAMAL
                      (almost to himself)
                 Well, Oxford has Broad Street,
                 Saint Aldates, Turl Street, Queen
                 Street, The High and Magdalene
                 Bridge- which is pronounced
                 Maudlin, so-

He stops as he hears the surprised laughter of the
audience.

                          PREM
                 I thought you hadn't been to UK.

                          JAMAL
                 Oh, I haven't. And it's not Leeds,
                 because that's Elland Road,
                 Kirkgate Market, Commercial
                 Street, St Peter's-

                          PREM
                      (icy)
                 - what *might* it be then, Jamal?

                          JAMAL
                 Well, I don't think it's
                 Cambridge.

                          PREM
                 *Cambridge* Circus is not in
                 Cambridge? Dare I ask why?

                    JAMAL
          Too obvious. There's definitely an
          Oxford Circus in London, and
          there's a rowing race between
          Oxford and Cambridge so there's
          probably a Cambridge Circus too.
          I'll go for D) London.

                    PREM
          That's the logic that's got him
          this far, Ladies and Gentlemen.
          Who are we to argue? So. Jamal. D.
          Apka final jawab?

                    JAMAL
               (shrugs)
          If the Gods are with me...Final
          answer. D.

The lights dim, the music swells as Prem pushes the
button on his computer.

                    PREM
          Computer-ji, D lock kiya-jaye.

More portentous music.

                    PREM (CONT'D)
          It's been a rollercoaster ride all
          the way, a pleasure to have you on
          the show, my friend, but I'm sorry
          to say that you're....incredibly,
          absolutely right!

Huge cheers and applause. Even Jamal laughs at this. He
cannot quite believe it himself.

                    PREM (CONT'D)
          Ladies and Gentlemen, Jamal Malik,
          the man with two and a half
          million rupees!

More applause. Prem hands him a cheque. Jamal looks at
it. Laughs again.

                    PREM (CONT'D)
          A few hours ago, you were fetching
          tea for the phone-wallahs. Now you
          are richer than they ever will
          ever be. What a player, Ladies and
          Gentleman! What a player.

The lights dim, the music swells. Prem consults his
computer.

                                              (CONTINUED)

123     CONTINUED: (2)                                      123

                              PREM (CONT'D)
                    For five million rupees, my
                    friend: who invented the revolver?
                    Was it A) Samuel Colt, B) Bruce
                    Browning, C Dan Wesson or D) James
                    Revolver?

Dramatic pause.


124     INT. HOTEL. NIGHT.                                  124

A flash of Salim shooting Maman. Another flash of Salim
in the doorway, holding the pistol up to Jamal's head.


125     INT. STUDIO. NIGHT.                                 125

                              JAMAL
                         (suddenly)
                    A). Samuel Colt.

                              PREM
                    A). Samuel Colt. Are you sure?

Jamal nods.

                              PREM (CONT'D)
                    Final answer?

                              JAMAL
                    Final answer.

The music swells again. Prem presses his computer.

                              PREM
                    You had two and a half million
                    rupees. If I may-?

He holds out his hand. Jamal hands him back the cheque.
He tears the cheque in two.

                              PREM (CONT'D)
                    Ladies and Gentlemen, the chai-          *
                    wallah has done it again! D. Is
                    right! Incredible!

Cheers and applause from the audience.

125A    INT. INSPECTOR'S OFFICE. NIGHT.                          125A

                    INSPECTOR
          Not that incredible. You'd just
          murdered somebody with a Colt 45,
          after all.

                    JAMAL
          It was self-defence.

                    INSPECTOR
          Let's call it manslaughter, then,
          shall we?

126     INT. STUDIO. NIGHT.                                      126

                    PREM
          Getting hot in here, isn't it?

                    JAMAL
               (genuinely)
          Are you nervous?

The audience laugh. Prem is momentarily flustered.

                    PREM
          What? Am *I* nervous? You're the one
          who's in the hot seat, my friend.

                    JAMAL
          Oh. Yes. Sorry.

More laughter.

127     INT. GALLERY. NIGHT.                                     127

                    DIRECTOR
          Bloody hell. He's got Prem on the
          run...

128     INT. STUDIO. NIGHT.                                      128

Music, lights. Prem presses his computer.

                    PREM
          What sports do you play?

                    JAMAL
          None.

                                              (CONTINUED)

>                         PREM
>           None. Oh, dear, oh dear, oh dear.
>           Not to worry, there's only ten
>           million rupees at stake... Which
>           cricketer has scored the most
>           first class centuries in history.
>           Was it A) Sachin Tendulkar, B)
>           Ricky Ponting, C) Michael Slater,
>           D) Jack Hobbs.

Prem allows the question to sink in.

>                         PREM (CONT'D)
>           You've got a cheque for five
>           million rupees in your hands.
>           You've still got two life-lines,
>           Phone A Friend and 50/50. For ten
>           million rupees: pay, play, or bail
>           out. It's still an option.
>           Remember, if you get the answer
>           wrong, you will lose everything
>           like that.

He clicks his fingers.

>                         PREM (CONT'D)
>           Are you sure you want to do this?

129    EXT. CRICKET GROUND. DAY.                                 129

An Indian batsman hits a nicely-timed stroke, heads down
the wicket for a single. Turns. The other batsman is
taking a second run. The Indian tries to halt the other
batsman with a shout, then succumbs to the inevitable and
charges down the wicket. A fielder hurls the ball at the
stumps. The bails fly off.

130    INT. STUDIO. NIGHT.                                       130

>                         JAMAL
>           I'll play.

Tense laughter from the audience. Prem holds up the
cheque. Jamal nods. Prem tears it up slowly. Allows the
pieces to fall to the floor.

>                         PREM
>           The dreams of so many. On the
>           floor.

131     EXT. TOWER BLOCK. DAY.                          131

Jamal is riding the construction lift to the top of a
high building, still just a shell but buzzing with
carpenters, bricklayers, cable-layers. The lift stops at
the top. Jamal gets out. Looks around. He is miles up.
Alone.

                    SALIM
        Jamal!

Jamal looks around. There is Salim standing on the edge
of the building. He saunters over to Jamal, his arms
outstretched in theatrical greeting. He is groomed,
expensively dressed with the best mobile money can buy
dangling from a gold chain around his neck.

                SALIM (CONT'D)
        God is good, bhai. God is good.

He tries to embrace Jamal. With as much force as he can
muster, Jamal punches him in the face. Salim takes it.
Stands there. Wipes blood from his lip. Gets another
punch. Then another and another, not even defending
himself, until he is being beaten back by a raging Jamal
towards the edge of the building. Finally, he tries to
reason with Jamal

                SALIM (CONT'D)
        Maman's boys were after us. Had to
        skip.

Jamal keeps on beating him back.

                    JAMAL
        Liar.

                    SALIM
        Left a message at reception.
        Waited weeks for you in Nagpur.

                    JAMAL
        There was no message at reception.

                    SALIM
        Bhai, I left a message.

Salim opens his arms, defenceless. It would take one,
small push to send him over the edge. There is a moment,
when Jamal might. He even has his hands on his chest.

                    JAMAL
        I will never forgive you.

                                        (CONTINUED)

131    CONTINUED:                                              131

                              SALIM
            I know.

The fury in Jamal subsides minutely. Finally, he turns
away with a roar of frustration. Salim hangs his head.


131A   EXT. TOWER BLOCK. LATER.                                131A

Jamal and Salim are sitting on the very edge of the
building. They can see for miles across the city. Salim
has rediscovered his attitude.

                              SALIM
            Can you believe it? This was our
            slum. We lived just there, huh?
            Now it is business, apartments,
            call centres...Fuck USA, fuck
            China. India is at the centre of
            the world, now, bhai. And I am at
            the centre of the centre, Jamal.
            This is all Javed-bhai's.

                              JAMAL
            Javed Mehta? The Gangster from our
            slum? You work for him?

                              SALIM
            Who else would protect us from
            Maman's gang, huh?

                              JAMAL
            What do you do for him?

                              SALIM
            Anything he asks.

Salim's mobile rings. Salim is immediately subservient on
the phone. Rings off.

                              SALIM (CONT'D)
            He is coming. You must go. My
            card.

He hands Jamal a card.

                              JAMAL
            What for?

                              SALIM
            You think I am going to let you
            out of my sight again, little
            brother? You stay with me now. Ab
            phut!

                                              (CONTINUED)

131A     CONTINUED:                                          131A

                              JAMAL
                    Salim, where's Latika?

                              SALIM
                    Still? She's gone, Jamal. Long
                    gone. Now go. Quick.

        Jamal gets up, hurries away, hidden behind piles of
        building materials just as Javed appears in his flash
        suit and jewelry. Three of his young henchmen walk
        alongside.


132     INT. SALIM'S APARTMENT.  NIGHT.                       132

        Jamal is asleep on a mattress on the floor of a smart
        apartment. A mobile phone rings. The muffled sound of
        Salim talking quietly next door. Then, Salim creeps into
        the room, checks to see Jamal is asleep, unlocks a desk
        drawer and brings out his pistol. He puts it in a hold-
        all and goes out the front door. Jamal's eyes snap open.
        He has seen it all.

                              JAMAL V/O
                    Slum dogs never sleep, only nap.
                    He would disappear for a couple of
                    days and come back changed.
                    Sometimes elated-


133     INT. SALIM'S APARTMENT. NIGHT.                        133

        The door bangs open and a giggling-drunk, half-naked Bar
        Girl drags the sleeping Jamal up and into the bathroom.

                              BAR GIRL
                    He has flipped! I can't do
                    anything with him....

        Salim is in the bath, bathing, literally, in money.

                              SALIM
                    Look at it, bhai, look at it!


134     INT. SALIM'S APARTMENT. DAWN.                         134

                              JAMAL V/O
                    Sometimes the opposite.

        Jamal creeps towards Salim's bedroom door. He pushes it
        open a fraction to see Salim crouched on the floor in
        prayer, sobbing quietly.

                                                      (CONTINUED)

134    CONTINUED:                                            134

                         SALIM
                      (whispering)
              Aé khuda mujhé baksh dé mainé
              bahut gunaah kiyé hain....

                         JAMAL V/O
              But younger brothers don't
              interfere. Mostly.


135    EXT. SALIM'S APARTMENT. DAY.                          135

       Salim comes out of his apartment block. Gets into his
       jeep. Drives off. Doesn't notice Jamal in the motor
       rickshaw that pulls out and follows him.


136    EXT. JAVED'S BUNGALOW. DAY.                           136

       Salim approaches a gate-house to a large bungalow. The
       Door-Keeper nods to him, rings a bell. From the rickshaw,
       Jamal watches a woman come to the door. Latika. Eighteen,
       completely beautiful and rich. She hands Salim a package
       and goes back inside. Salim gets in his jeep and drives
       away.


137    EXT. JAVED'S BUNGALOW. DAY.                           137

       Jamal approaches the Door-Keeper's gate-house.

                         JAMAL
              Baba, I am the new cook from the
              agency. A thousand apologies, I am
              late for the Memsaab.

       The Door-Keeper grunts and goes inside. After a brief
       pause, he returns.

                         DOOR-KEEPER
              She doesn't know anything about
              any cook. There's supposed to be a
              dishwasher being delivered. Know
              anything about that?

                         JAMAL
              Baba, I am your dishwasher!

       The Door-keeper grunts at this attempt at humour. Latika
       appears at the gate.

                         LATIKA
              Haven't I told you, don't
              interrupt when I'm watching-

137     CONTINUED:                                          137

She looks at Jamal. Is silenced briefly.

                    LATIKA (CONT'D)
               - come inside. I'll show you the
               kitchen.


138     INT. KITCHEN. DAY.                                  138

Latika and Jamal go into the kitchen. *Who Wants To Be A
Millionaire* plays on the tv in the background. She turns
and hugs him tight. They laugh with happiness.

                    LATIKA
               (delighted)
               Jamal, Jamal, look at you...!

Their heads are close, they might kiss. Then Latika turns
away, stares out of the window.

                    LATIKA (CONT'D)
               Aré wa, Jamal....

Jamal smiles hopefully at her. But there is sadness in
her now. She takes her sunglasses off, rubs her eyes.
There is a bruise there.

                    JAMAL
               You've hurt your eye.

                    LATIKA
               Why are you here?

                    JAMAL
               To see you.

                    LATIKA
               Well. You see me.

She stands there, challenging. On the tv, somebody is
winning money.

                    JAMAL
               Why does everyone love this
               programme?

                    LATIKA
               It's the chance to escape, isn't
               it? Walk into another life.
               Doesn't everyone want that?

                    JAMAL
               You have another life. A rich one.

                                              (CONTINUED)

> LATIKA
> Who'd have thought it possible? A
> slum dog, with all this.

> JAMAL
> Are you happy?

> LATIKA
> I have five star food, five star
> clothes. I sleep in a bed, not on
> the street. From where we come
> from, Jamal, that is happiness.

> JAMAL
> You don't look so happy with a
> black eye.

> LATIKA
> You turn up here out of nowhere,
> telling me I'm not happy: how dare
> you?

Voices at the gate-house.

> LATIKA (CONT'D)
> God, Javed will kill you. Here.

> JAMAL
> Javed? You are with *him*?

She throws him an apron. He gets it on just in time for
Javed to walk in. Jamal turns away.

> JAVED
> First you want a dishwasher, now a
> bloody cook-

> LATIKA
> -I just thought-

> JAVED
> - chup. The cricket's on.

Javed changes channel and dials on his mobile.

> JAVED (CONT'D)
> Why do you always watch that shit?
> Huh? I'm already a millionaire.

He laughs at his own joke. Turns to Jamal.

> JAVED (CONT'D)
> Well, come on then, *Cook*. I'm
> hungry. Get me a sandwich.

138     CONTINUED: (2)

                          JAMAL
                 Immediately, Sir.

Javed stares at Jamal a moment, trying to place a face he
vaguely recognises. Then the Bookie comes on the line and
he turns back to the television.

                          JAVED
                 Atcha...

Latika hurries around the kitchen getting out bread and
condiments, whispering while Javed talks on the phone.

                          JAMAL
                 Come away with me.

                          LATIKA
                 Chutiyé. Away where? And live on
                 what? What can you provide? What
                 have you *got*, Jamal?

                          JAMAL
                 Love.

                          JAVED
                      (on the mobile)
                 ..yeah. He's on eighty-five. I
                 want four lakh on him making a
                 century. What are you
                 giving?...Okay, make it five lakh.

Javed pours himself a glass of whisky, never taking his
eyes from the television.

                          TV COMMENTATOR
                 We are watching history unfold
                 today at the Wankhedé Stadium as
                 Sachin Tendulkar carves his way
                 towards another magnificent
                 century and the record books. His
                 thirty-eighth century- the most by
                 any Indian cricketer ever...

                          LATIKA
                 Love. That will feed us, will it?

                          JAMAL
                 It won't buy you a new dishwasher,
                 but it might make you happy.

                          LATIKA
                 Where have you been? Get in the
                 real world, Jamal.

                                              (CONTINUED)

138    CONTINUED: (3)                                              138

                              JAMAL
              You and me. That is the real
              world. Come away with me.

Latika snatches the sandwich from him and gives it to
Javed. Goes back to Jamal, whispers under cover of
putting condiments away.

                              LATIKA
              You're crazy.

                              JAMAL
              Salim will help us.

                              LATIKA
              Salim? You still believe in Salim?
              Jamal...I'll be gone soon, anyway.
              Bombay's got too dangerous for-

She indicates Javed.

                              JAMAL
              Where?

                              LATIKA
              You think he'd tell me?

                              JAVED
              Straight bat, straight bat,
              dammit.

Then the batsman at the other end calls to take a second
run.

                              JAVED (CONT'D)
              No! A single!

Tendulkar seems to agree, tries to halt the other batsman
with a shout, then succumbs to the inevitable and charges
down the wicket. A fielder hurls the ball at the stumps.
The bails fly off.

                              JAVED (CONT'D)
              No, no, no! stupid ben chod
              idiot...

He flings his glass of whisky at the television. Suddenly
tastes what he has been eating.

                              JAVED (CONT'D)
              And what is this shit supposed to
              be, mader chod? Get out. Get out!

                                              (CONTINUED)

Javed throws the sandwich at him and slams out of the
room. His footsteps can be heard stomping into another
room.

                         LATIKA
              Now go, before he kills us both.

She leads Jamal to the door.

                         JAVED
              Latika, where's my bloody shirt?
              The Armani.

Latika shouts over her shoulder.

                         LATIKA
              Coming!

Back to Jamal.

                         LATIKA (CONT'D)
                    (whispered)
              You want to do something for me?

                         JAMAL
              Anything.

                         LATIKA
              Then forget me.

                         JAMAL
              I'll wait at VT station. Five
              o'clock every day until you come.

She shakes her head.

                         JAMAL (CONT'D)
              I love you.

                         LATIKA
              So what, Jamal? So what? (loudly)
              Now, get out and tell your no-good
              agency not to send anybody else
              until they've learnt to cook. You
              hear?

She slams the door. Hurries back into the kitchen, throws
Javed's plate into the sink. The Door-keeper comes in.

                         DOOR-KEEPER
              Madam, your dishwasher has
              arrived.

Leaning over the sink, Latika weeps silently.

139     INT. SALIM'S APARTMENT. NIGHT.     

Salim has his hand around Jamal's throat.

> SALIM
> Why can't you let it alone? You
> want money, I'll give you money.
> Girls? I can get you girls.

> JAMAL
> You know what I want.

> SALIM
> You're like some crazy man- you're
> obsessed.

> JAMAL
> She is my destiny, Salim.

> SALIM
> Know what your destiny is, crazy
> boy? A bullet between the eyes.
> And after that, he'll kill her. Is
> that what you want? Huh?

> JAMAL
> Me, I don't care. Latika? She's
> already half dead.

Salim takes his hand away from Jamal's neck.

> SALIM
> Yes. About that, you are right.

> JAMAL
> You sold her.

> SALIM
> (fierce)
> I didn't sell her. Javed wanted
> her. He gets what he wants.

He turns away bitterly.

> SALIM (CONT'D)
> She's doing alright. Get it into
> your thick head, Jamal. She's not
> yours and she never will be.

140          INT. STUDIO. NIGHT.                                    140

                              PREM
                    Time for a commercial break,
                    Ladies and Gentlemen. I know, I
                    know, I can't stand the tension
                    either. Don't even think about
                    leaving your seat. We'll be back.

The lights flick back on. Prem slumps back in his chair.

                              PREM (CONT'D)
                    You've got the luck of the devil,
                    yaar, I'll give you that.

                              JAMAL
                    I- I need to-

                              PREM
                    Oh, the toilet. Sure. Naveed,
                    Jamal wants the bog.

The Floor Manager and a Security Guard usher Jamal off-
stage. Prem looks up at the gallery, raises his eyes at
the Director. Some show. Then he gathers himself and
heads off-stage.


141          INT. CHHATRAPATI SHIVAJI TERMINUS. DAY.                141

The clock reads five oh three. Jamal stands on the
footbridge. Humanity washes around him. His eyes dart
around, frightened to miss her. Checks the clock again.
Six. The platform is almost deserted. He wanders away.


142          INT. CORRIDOR. NIGHT.                                  142

Prem wanders down the corridor followed by a Security
Guard. Another Security Guard is waiting at the entrance
to the toilet. Prem goes in, leaving the two Guards in
the corridor.


143          INT. CHHATRAPATI SHIVAJI TERMINUS. DAY.                143

Jamal stands on the footbridge gazing down at the hordes
of commuters. Five o'clock, five fifteen, five thirty.
Six. Jamal rests his head against the railings.

144    INT. TOILET. NIGHT.                                144

Jamal is in one of the cubicles. Prem goes to the urinal.
Unzips.

                    PREM
          A guy from the slums becomes a
          millionaire overnight. You know
          the only other person who's done
          that? Me. I know what it's like. I
          know what you've been through.

                    JAMAL O/S
          I'm not going to become a
          milionaire. I don't know the
          answer.

                    PREM
              (laughs)
          You've said that before, yaar.

Prem finishes pissing. Goes over to the washbasins, runs
the taps and washes his hands.

                    JAMAL O/S
          No, I really don't.

                    PREM
          What? You can't take the money and
          run now. You're on the edge of
          history, kid!

                    JAMAL O/S
          I don't see what else I can do.

                    PREM
          Maybe it is written, my friend.
          You're going to win this. Trust
          me, you're going to win.

Prem leaves. Jamal flushes and comes out of the cubicle.
Goes to the washbasins. In the mist on the mirror above
the taps is written the letter "B". Jamal stares at it.
Gradually it fades, leaving only the growing fury on his
face staring back at him.

145    INT. STUDIO. NIGHT.                                145

Jamal stalks back onto the set. Sits down in his chair.
Stares at Prem who looks unconcernedly back.

(CONTINUED)

145     CONTINUED:                                              145

                              TALKBACK V/O
                     Twenty seconds.


145A    INT. CHHATRAPATI SHIVAJI TERMINUS. DAY.           145A

        The digital clocks show five fifteen. Shoving the
        descending river of people out of his way, the seventeen
        year-old Jamal is forging a path up steps that cross the
        platforms. He pushes to the middle of the footbridge and
        leans out on the side railings. He scans the sea of
        people, desperately. Then he sees her: the eighteen year-
        old Latika, heart-stoppingly beautiful, over the other
        side of the station. A world away. She is scanning the
        crowd, as wired as he is.

                                JAMAL
                     Latika! Latika!

        But though he is screaming her name, his voice is
        swallowed by the noise around him. Then he sees two
        thuggish-looking men also fighting a way towards her.

                            JAMAL (CONT'D)
                     Latika!

        Frightened now, he fights his way down the steps, one
        figure against an army of white-robed people. He gets to
        the bottom of the steps, is making progress against the
        tide. But so are the two men. Jamal is now on the same
        platform. Shouts her name again. She turns with a smile.
        But the two Thugs leap through a train onto her platform.
        She sees them, starts running, is lost in the crowd.
        Jamal runs off along the platform after Latika.

                            JAMAL (CONT'D)
                     Latika! Latika!


        By the time Jamal has fought himself to where Latika was-
        she is gone. He whirls around, mad with frustration.

                            JAMAL (CONT'D)
                     Latika! Latika!


146     OMITTED                                               146


147     EXT. CHHATRAPATI SHIVAJI TERMINUS. DAY.            147

        Latika is jumping the tracks, crossing in front of
        trains. But the Thugs are gaining on her. He brings her
        down and drags her across to Javed's waiting Mercedes.

                                                    (CONTINUED)

Salim is standing by the car. Jamal pushes through the crowds just in time to see Salim bundling her into the car.

                         JAMAL
          Salim!

Salim spits disgustedly on the ground. Gets in. Latika twists her head to see Jamal as the car skids off. Jamal screams with hopeless fury.


148     INT. STUDIO. NIGHT.                                      148

                         TALKBACK V/O
               Fifteen seconds.

Jamal and Prem stare at each other. Prem smiles.

                         PREM
               Do the right thing and in
               approximately three minutes you
               will be as famous as me.

                         TALKBACK V/O
               Ten seconds.

                         PREM
               And as rich as me.

                         TALKBACK V/O
               Five seconds.

                         PREM
               Almost.

                         TALKBACK V/O
               Four, three...

                         PREM
               From rags to Raja. It's your
               destiny.

                         TALKBACK V/O
               ...we're on.

Applause from the audience.

                         PREM
               Welcome back to Who Wants to Be A
               Millionaire? In the chair tonight
               is Jamal Malik- as if we don't
               know!
                         (MORE)


                                                          (CONTINUED)

                                        PREM (CONT'D)
                          In an amazing run, Jamal has
                          already five million rupees but,
                          not content with that, has chosen
                          to gamble for one Crore- that's
                          ten million million rupees. What a
                          player! The question one more
                          time: Which cricketer has scored
                          the most first class centuries in
                          history. Was it A) Sachin
                          Tendulkar, B) Ricky Ponting, C)
                          Michael Slater, D) Jack Hobbs.

                                        JAMAL
                          I know it isn't Sachin Tendulkar.

                                        PREM
                          That's a start. So, it could be
                          Ricky Ponting, Jack Hobbs or
                          Michael Slater.

                                        JAMAL
                          I'll use a life-line. Fifty-fifty.

                                        PREM
                          Okay. Computer, take away two
                          wrong answers.

Music swells, lights dim.

                                        PREM (CONT'D)
                          Well, you were right about Sachin
                          Tendulkar. The computer has taken
                          away A) Sachin Tendulkar and C)
                          Michael Slater. That leaves you a
                          fifty-fifty choice, Jamal. B)
                          Ricky Ponting or D) Jack Hobbs.
                          What do you think? Decision time.
                          For half a million rupees. Your
                          answer: B) Ricky Ponting or D)
                          Jack Hobbs.

A hideous, never-ending pause while Jamal stares into
Prem's eyes.

                                        JAMAL
                          D.

A barely perceptible jump from Prem.

                                        PREM
                          You sure? Not B) Ricky Ponting?
                          The Australian? Great cricketer.

                                        JAMAL
                          D. Jack Hobbs.

                                                      (CONTINUED)

>                    PREM
>          Do you *know*?

Jamal shakes his head.

>                    PREM (CONT'D)
>          So it could be B, Ricky Ponting?

>                    JAMAL
>          Or D. Jack Hobbs.

>                    PREM
>          Final Answer?

>                    JAMAL
>          Final Answer. D.

A just-perceptible narrowing of the eyes.

>                    PREM
>          Computer-ji D lock kiya-jaye.

Prem turns to the computer. Music. Lights.

>                    PREM (CONT'D)
>          With one hundred and ninety- seven
>          first class centuries, the answer
>          is...D. Jack Hobbs!

The audience go wild. Prem's smile is thin.

>                    PREM (CONT'D)
>          Jamal Malik, Crorepati!

The camera goes off Prem for a second. He mimes a
disgusted spit. Then he is back on.

>                    PREM (CONT'D)
>          I cannot believe what I am seeing
>          here, tonight, Ladies and
>          Gentlemen....So, are you ready for
>          the final question for two Crore
>          rupees- twenty million rupees?

>                    JAMAL
>          Not really, but...maybe it is
>          written, no?

>                    PREM
>          Maybe, indeed. Okay, okay. For
>          twenty million rupees, the final
>          question on *Who Wants to be a
>          Millionaire?*

148     CONTINUED: (3)

The lights dim again, the portentous music increases.
Suddenly a klaxon sounds. The audience burst into nervous
laughter and groans. Prem laughs.

                    PREM (CONT'D)
          Ohhhhh! Just when I thought I
          would need a pacemaker fitted,
          we're out of time! What a show,
          Ladies and Gentlemen, what a show.
          Join us tomorrow night to see if
          Jamal Malik has made the biggest
          mistake of his life or has just
          won the biggest prize in the
          history of Indian
          television....Same place, same
          time. You wouldn't dare miss it.
          Goodnight!

Applause. The studio lights come up. Prem switches off
his smile as fast as the cameras switch off. Gets up and
pulls out his mobile.


149     EXT. JAVED'S BUNGALOW. DAY.                                      149

Waving a kitchen knife in on hand, a desperate Jamal
slams through the gates of Javed's bungalow, the
objecting Doorkeeper running along behind. He bangs open
the front door.

                    JAMAL
          Latika!


150     INT. JAVED'S BUNGALOW. DAY.                                      150

Stops dead. The place has been stripped of everything.
Not a single thing remains. Jamal runs into another room.
As empty as the first. He stops in his tracks.

                    DOOR-KEEPER
          Told you.

                    JAMAL
          Where? Where is she?

                    DOOR-KEEPER
          Dunno.

He grabs the Door-keeper by the shirt-collar, slams him
up against the wall. Holds the knife against his throat.

                    JAMAL
          Where?

                                                          (CONTINUED)

                                         DOOR-KEEPER
                              I don't know! Wouldn't say, would
                              they? They had to get out fast.
                              The police. Honestly.

                    Jamal lets go of the Door-keeper. Goes hopelessly to the
                    window. On the window sill is a phone. He picks it up.
                    There is a dial tone. Jamal rummages in his trouser
                    pocket. Gets out the battered card with Salim's details
                    on. Dials. Salim picks up.

                                         JAMAL
                              Where are you? Where is she?


150A      INT. JAVED'S SAFE HOUSE. SALIM'S ROOM. DAY.                    150A

          Salim is stalking around his room in Javed's new house.
          Hold-alls of clothes and possessions lie around the room.
          A chest of drawers sits with its drawers open, still
          empty.

                                         SALIM
                              Where you'll never find her. Or
                              me. You could have joined us, you
                              bloody idiot, been one of us.
                              You've lost everything now.
                              Everything.

          Cuts the call off and slings the phone in a drawer. Takes
          the gun from his waist, and throws that in too. Slams the
          drawer shut with as much force as he can.


150B      INT. JAVED'S BUNGALOW. DAY.                                    150B

                                         JAMAL
                              Salim...!

          The line goes dead. Jamal slides to the floor...


151       INT. SALIM'S APARTMENT. NIGHT.                                 151

          ...the camera pulls out from Jamal's face revealing that
          Jamal is sitting on the floor of Salim's apartment. In
          the background can be heard the sound of the television.
          Jamal looks at the knife in his hand, wonders what he
          might do with it. The sound of Prem's voice on the tv.

                                         PREM O/S
                              ...if you want a chance to play
                              *Who Wants to be a Millionaire*,
                              call now...!

151     CONTINUED:


        Jamal looks up. Stares at the tv.


152     INT. STUDIO. BACKSTAGE. NIGHT.                          152

                            PREM
                    This way, Jamal, this way. Great
                    show, my friend. See you tomorrow,
                    huh?

        In the half-light, Prem guides him to a stage door.


153     EXT. STUDIO. BACKSTAGE. NIGHT.                          153

        Jamal steps outside the backstage door. Leans on the rail
        and takes a huge breath. Immediately, a blanket is thrown
        over his head and two police men bundle him into the back
        of a police van. The Director joins Prem at the back-
        stage door as the van pulls away, sirens screaming.

                            DIRECTOR
                    What's going on?

                            PREM
                    He's a cheat.

                            DIRECTOR
                    This was you? You called them?

        Prem shrugs.

                            DIRECTOR (CONT'D)
                    How d'you know he's cheating?

                            PREM
                    Oh, come on! Of course he is. He's
                    a bloody village boy. Even when I
                    fed him the wrong answer the
                    little shit got it right.

        Director stares at him.

                            DIRECTOR
                    You gave him an answer?

                            PREM
                    Well, I didn't exactly-

        The Director walks away shaking his head. In the doorway,
        Nita is standing there, watching.

                            PREM (CONT'D)
                    Nita?

                                                        (CONTINUED)

153    CONTINUED:


        But she too turns and walks away.


154     INT. INSPECTOR'S OFFICE. DAY.                      154

                              INSPECTOR
                    It is all bizarrely plausible. And
                    yet...

                              JAMAL
                    Because I am a slum dog, chai-          *
                    wallah, I am a liar, right?

                              INSPECTOR
                    Most of you are.

        Srinivas comes hurrying in carrying a file, very pleased
        with himself.

                              CONSTABLE SRINIVAS
                    Shooting at Pila Street, October
                    19th...Maman Hossani....Victim
                    pronounced dead at scene. Suspects
                    absconded: two males, early teens,
                    one female, early teen.

        The Inspector takes the file. Stares at it. Shakes his
        head.

                              INSPECTOR
                    But you: you're not a liar, Mister
                    Malik, that is for sure. You are
                    too truthful.

        He turns to Srinivas.

                              INSPECTOR (CONT'D)
                    Thank you, Constable. All that
                    remains is to work out whether it
                    was manslaughter or murder. Ten
                    years, or life.

        The Young Constable sticks his head around the door.

                              YOUNG CONSTABLE
                    The Commissioner's here, Sir.

        The Inspector sighs. Gets up. Accompanied by Srinivas, he
        leaves the room. Jamal sits there. Lets his head drop.
        The camera floats from the room, down the dingy corridor
        and out through a window...

155   EXT. POLICE STATION. DAY.                              155

....alighting on a crowd of hundreds of people jostling
to get a view of the building. News crews are setting up
around them. A tv Reporter is doing a piece to camera.

                        TV REPORTER
                ....behind the walls of this
                police station lies the mystery
                all of India is talking about. Did
                Jamal Malik, an uneducated,
                eighteen year-old boy from the
                slums of Mumbai win one Crore
                rupees by fair means or foul? And
                in the crowds all around me there
                is an even bigger question. Will
                he be back on the show tonight to
                play for twenty million rupees...


156   OMITTED                                                156


156A  INT. POLICE OFFICE. DAY.                              156A

The Commissioner is waiting in the outer office.

                    COMMISSIONER OF POLICE
                So? Have you charged him yet?

                        INSPECTOR
                I- progress is being made sir.

                    COMMISSIONER OF POLICE
                Progress? Have you *charged* him?

                        INSPECTOR
                No, Sir.

The Commissioner dumps a copy of the *Times of India* down
on the desk. Then the *Hindustan Times*, the *Amar Ujala* and
the *Afternoon Dispatch* thump down after them. All have
photos of Jamal on *Who Wants to be a Millionaire* on the
front page.

                    COMMISSIONER OF POLICE
                And if that isn't enough for
                you...

He motions the Inspector to come over to the window.

Lifts the blind. The Inspector hurries over. Looks
alarmed.

                                              (CONTINUED)

                             INSPECTOR
            That's-?

                     COMMISSIONER OF POLICE
            - yes, yes! The boy's a bloody
            hero with every beggar and thief
            in the city. We're in danger of
            looking very stupid, here,
            Inspector.

                             INSPECTOR
            Whilst I'm not convinced he
            actually cheated, I have got-

The Inspector brandishes the file.

                     COMMISSIONER OF POLICE
            - Prem Kumar himself- a man of
            great standing and integrity- said
            the kid was a liar and a cheat.
            What more do you need?

The Inspector pauses.

                             INSPECTOR
            A liar.

Then he puts the file behind his back. Srinivas frowns.

                       INSPECTOR (CONT'D)
            Indeed, sir.

Srinivas coughs pointedly. Gets a steely look from the
Inspector. The Commissioner has been staring out of the
window at the crowds. Turns back to them.

                     COMMISIONER OF POLICE
            He's in for fraud, so you charge
            him for fraud. Fast. Or you'll
            find yourself on traffic duty at
            the Gateway of India. Understand?

                             INSPECTOR
             Yes, sir.

The Commissioner walks out.

                     CONSTABLE SRINIVAS
            Sir-?

                             INSPECTOR
Not a word, Srinivas.

157    INT. JAVED'S SAFE-HOUSE. SITTING ROOM. NIGHT.    157

A cheek scarred by disfiguring knife scars. Pulling back
we see it is Latika, staring frozen at Jamal on the
television news. A palatial living room. Dealing cards to
Salim, is Javed Khan. A couple of Bar Girls giggle next
to Javed and a couple of his Thugs. Pouring drinks at a
sideboard is Latika. Javed glances up at the screen,
clearly not recognising Jamal on a clip from Who Wants to
be a Millionaire. Salim, too is staring, wide-eyed at the
tv. Javed picks up the remote, doesn't even notice and
switches over to a music channel. Latika hurries out.

                    JAVED
          What about my bloody whisky,
          woman?

But she has already gone. He growls after her.

                    JAVED (CONT'D)
          Hey, Salim.

He motions Salim to get him a drink. Javed's mobile rings
as Salim goes over to the sideboard. Shifts a bottle to
the back.

                    SALIM
          We're out. I'll just get- Syed.

Salim smiles faintly at the image of Jamal and hurries
out.

158    INT . JAVED'S SAFE-HOUSE. SALIM'S ROOM. NIGHT.    158

A drawer opens. Inside is Salim's pistol. And a phone-
the same one he threw in there months ago. Salim stares
at both for a long time. Finally, picks up the gun and
phone.

                    SALIM
              (to himself)
          Final answer?

He finds this faintly amusing.

159    INT. JAVED'S SAFE-HOUSE. KITCHEN. NIGHT.    159

Latika sits in the kitchen, staring at the tv, tears
running down her cheeks. A reporter is talking in front
of an enlarged photograph of Jamal.

                                        (CONTINUED)

159    CONTINUED:                                              159

Latika wipes away the tears quickly as Salim comes in. He locks the door behind him. Stares at the tv.

> SALIM
> That boy. He will never give up.
> Never.

He shakes his head.

> SALIM (CONT'D)
> Crazy chutiyé.

Salim approaches Latika. She flinches as he walks towards her. He puts some car keys in front of her.

> SALIM (CONT'D)
> Ja. Go.

> LATIKA
> But-

> SALIM
> - just drive. There won't be
> another chance. Go.

Latika takes the keys. Hesitates.

> LATIKA
> He'll kill you.

Salim smiles, shakes his head.

> SALIM
> It is not written.

> JAVED O/S
> Salim!

Salim goes to the back door. Unlocks it. Opens it for her.

> LATIKA
> Salim, I....can't.

Salim points at the television.

> SALIM
> You have to. It'll take you two
> hours if you drive fast. Here.

He holds out his mobile phone.

> SALIM (CONT'D)
> For God's sake, hold on to it.

(CONTINUED)

CONTINUED: (2)

Latika takes it. Salim takes hold of both sides of her
head for a moment.

>                    SALIM (CONT'D)
>              For what I have done, please
>              forgive me.

Salim releases her.

>                    SALIM (CONT'D)
>              Go. Have a good life.

Salim puts his hands together in blessing. She leaves.
Salim shuts the door, locks it. Smiles.

160      INT. INSPECTOR'S OFFICE. NIGHT.                     160

Jamal is dozing in the chair. He wakes with a shout.
Srinivas has just thrown a bucket of water in his face.
He unlocks the handcuffs. Jamal looks up at him. Srinivas
shrugs.

>                 CONSTABLE SRINIVAS
>              You're back on the show.

161      INT. BACKSTAGE. NIGHT.                              161

The audience for *Who Wants to be a Millionaire* are
standing in line. They are being body-searched by police.
Mobiles are being confiscated and put in bags.

162      INT. BACKSTAGE. NIGHT.                              162

Gaffers make last-minute adjustments to the lights
shining on the empty chairs in the middle of the set.
Camera positions are checked by the Floor Manager.

163      INT. POLICE OFFICE. NIGHT.                          163

Srinivas walks Jamal through the police office, past the
Inspector sitting at his desk, his arms behind his head,
pondering. He watches Jamal go and then asks:

>                 INSPECTOR OF POLICE
>              What happened? To the girl?
>              Latika?

Jamal stops.

(CONTINUED)

163     CONTINUED:                                              163

                              JAMAL
                    Who knows?

Jamal walks on. The Inspector watches him all the way.


164     INT. POLICE JEEP. NIGHT.                                164

Jamal sits in the back of the police jeep. It pulls out
of the police station car park into a sea of people all
cheering and shouting at the jeep. Jamal looks terrified.


165     INT. CAR. NIGHT.                                        165

Latika drives through the slums of Mumbai. She hoots her
horn furiously at a cart-driver ambling across the road.


166     INT. POLICE JEEP. NIGHT.                                166

The jeep stops at the lights and a beggar wanders up,
tapping on the windscreen. The beggar studies Jamal's
face for a second, then starts shouting and pointing at
him.

                              BEGGAR
                    Crorepati! Crorepati!

Other beggars- just like the one Jamal used to be- join
him and start cheering and applauding. The jeep pulls
away.


167     OMITTED                                                 167


168     EXT. SLUM. NIGHT.                                       168

At the chai stall, everyone gathers around the tv,              *
watching.


169     EXT. ROADSIDE CHI HOUSE. NIGHT.                         169

A rickshaw parks up next to a hundred others. The Driver
leaps out, abandoning the irate business man in the back
and runs to the tv in the café.

170     INT. CALL CENTRE. NIGHT.                    170

The Manager walks into the aircraft hanger of a building.
Stops. Where is everyone? Then he sees everyone crowded
around the tv in the Recreation Room. Stalks over.

                         MANAGER
              Oi! Get back to work.

Then he sees Jamal's face on the tv.

                         MANAGER (CONT'D)
              The chai-*wallah*?                              *

171     EXT. ROADSIDE SHACKS. NIGHT.                171

All along the highway, one by one the televisions in a
hundred shacks flick on, silhouetting the family huddled
in front of it.

172     INT. STUDIO. BACKSTAGE. NIGHT.              172

In the half-light, Jamal is being powdered by Nita.

                         NITA
              Good luck.

Prem sneers.

                         TALKBACK V/O
              Two minutes.

She finishes powdering Jamal.

                         PREM
              Hey. Sweetheart. What about me?
              I'm sweating, here.

                         NITA
              You should be.

She dumps the powder compact in his hand.

                         PREM
              So. Tonight. The Calypso Bar.

                         NITA
              Not if you were the only man in
              the world.

She walks off.

(CONTINUED)

172      CONTINUED:                                              172

                           PREM
                    (genuinely puzzled)
                 But I am the only man in the
                 world.

173      EXT. MUMBAI STREET. NIGHT.                               173

         The traffic is gridlocked. Latika is pumping the horn.

                          LATIKA
                 Come on, come on!

         She glances out of the window, sees one of the roadside
         shacks with the television on. Gets out of the car and
         runs to it.

173A     INT. COMMISSIONER'S OFFICE. NIGHT.                       173A

         The Commissioner grabs his phone.

                      COMMISSIONER OF POLICE
                 Get me the Inspector on the phone
                 now!

173B     INT. INSPECTOR'S OFFICE. NIGHT.                          173B

         The Inspector wanders into his office, still deep in
         thought. Switches on the television just as the
         *Millionaire* music starts. Sits. The phone rings.

174      OMITTED                                                  174

175      OMITTED                                                  175

176      OMITTED                                                  176

177      INT. STUDIO. NIGHT.                                      177

         Prem and Jamal walk on-stage. Blinding light. They take
         their seats to tumultuous applause.

                           PREM
                 Welcome back to *Who Wants to be a*
                 *Millionaire?* I can safely say that
                 tonight is the biggest night of
                 both of our lives, Ladies and
                 Gentlemen.
                          (MORE)
                                                        (CONTINUED)

177    CONTINUED:                                                177

                         PREM (CONT'D)
                Jamal Malik, the Call Centre
                worker from Mumbai has already won
                one Crore rupees, a cool ten
                million. Tonight, he can walk away
                with that in his pocket or make
                the biggest gamble in television
                history and go for the final
                question and a staggering twenty
                million rupees! Jamal, are you
                ready for that question?

                         JAMAL
                Yes.

The lights dim, the music rumbles. Prem pushes the button
on his computer. Pauses. Gets conversational.

                         PREM
                Big reader, are you Jamal? A lover
                of literature?

Nervous laughter from the audience. Jamal just shrugs.

                         JAMAL
                I can read.

Even more nervous laughter.

                         PREM
                Lucky! In Alexandre Dumas' book,
                The Three Musketeers, two of the
                musketeers are called Athos and
                Porthos. What was the name of the
                third musketeer. Was it A) Aramis,
                B) Cardinal Richelieu, C)
                D'Artagnan, D) Planchet.

An involuntary laugh comes out of Jamal's mouth.


178    INT. ROADSIDE SHACK. NIGHT.                               178

In the shack, sitting on an upturned oil drum, surrounded
by puzzled Indians in rags, a slow smile comes to
Latika's face.


179    OMITTED                                                   179


180    INT. STUDIO. NIGHT.                                       180

Camera on Prem.


                                                        (CONTINUED)

                              PREM
                    The final question, for twenty
                    million rupees: and he's smiling.
                    I guess you know the answer.

                              JAMAL
                    Would you believe it? I don't.

Jamal laughs. There's nothing else to do. The audience
groan.

                              PREM
                    You don't? So, you're going to
                    take the ten million and walk?

                              JAMAL
                    No.

                              PREM
                    No?

                              JAMAL
                    I'll play.

A gasp from the audience.

                              PREM
                    You just said you don't know the
                    answer. I heard that, right? You
                    do understand that if you get the
                    answer wrong, you lose everything?
                    Ten million rupees. A fortune,
                    Jamal.

A terrible pause.

                              JAMAL
                    I'd like to phone a friend.

                              PREM
                    We're going to the wire, Ladies
                    and Gentlemen, we are going to the
                    wire. The final Life-line. Here we
                    go....

181     INT. STUDIO. NIGHT.                            181

Prem presses his computer. Ominous rumble of drums. The
lights dim. A phone can be heard ringing, the amplified
sound echoing around the studio.

                              PREM
                    It's ringing.

(CONTINUED)

181     CONTINUED:                                          181

        The phone continues to ring.


182     INT. ROADSIDE SHACK. NIGHT.                         182

        Latika is staring at the television. Then an electric
        current seems to shoot through her and she is running,
        dodging the static traffic, street vendors, the odd cow,
        heading for her abandoned car. Hooting horns, shouting
        drivers. The phone rings on...


183     INT. STUDIO. NIGHT.                                 183

        And on...

                            PREM
                Doesn't look as if your friend is
                in, Jamal. Who is it?

                            JAMAL
                My brother's number, but-

                            PREM
                - the sort of brother who'd go for
                a walk on the twenty million rupee
                question?

                            JAMAL
                It's the only number I know.


184     INT. CAR. NIGHT.                                    184

        On the passenger seat of Latika's car, Salim's phone
        continues to ring...


185     INT. STUDIO. NIGHT.                                 185

        ...and ring.

                            PREM
                You're on your own, Jamal.

        Prem looks up at the gallery. The Director shakes his
        head, mimes cutting his throat.


186     INT. CAR. NIGHT.                                    186

        Latika wrestles the door open, grabs the phone.

187     INT. STUDIO. NIGHT.                                      187

Prem opens his mouth to speak. Then, out of the darkness
of the studio,

                    LATIKA V/O
          Hello?

A gasp from the audience.

                    LATIKA V/O (CONT'D)
          Hello? Jamal?

                    PREM
          Wow! That's cutting it fine. I'm
          guessing this isn't your brother.
          This is-

                    LATIKA V/O
          My name is Latika.

The first real smile of Jamal's adult life.


188     EXT. STUDIO. BACKSTAGE. NIGHT.                          188

A small smile spreads across the Inspector's face.

                    INSPECTOR
          *That's* why he's on the show.

He picks up his hat and hastens out of the room.


189     INT. JAVED'S SAFE-HOUSE. NIGHT.                         189

Javed pulls the Bar Girl from him, stares open-mouthed at
the television.

                    JAVED
          What the bloody-?

He pushes the girl off him. Gets to his feet.

                    JAVED (CONT'D)
          Latika! Salim!

190    INT. STUDIO/ INT. ROADSIDE SHACK. NIGHT.                190

                          PREM
              Okay! So, Latika, you want to hear
              the question one more time? And
              let's be clear about this. Twenty
              million rupees ride on your
              answer. You have thirty seconds.
              Jamal, please read out the
              question to Latika.

                          JAMAL
              Is that really you?

                          LATIKA V/O
              Yes.

                          PREM
              The question, Jamal.

                          JAMAL
              In Alexandre Dumas' book, The
              Three Musketeers, two of the
              musketeers are called Athos and
              Porthos. What was the name of the
              third musketeer. Was it A) Aramis,
              B) Cardinal Richelieu, C)
              D'Artagnan, D) Planchet.

    Silence. The electronic clock ticks loudly.

                          PREM
              Fifteen seconds.

                          JAMAL
              Where are you?

                          LATIKA V/O
              I'm- I'm safe.

                          PREM
              Ten seconds. So, Latika, what do
              you think?

    Silence.

                          PREM (CONT'D)
              Five, four, three, two, one.
              Time's up! Your answer.

                          LATIKA V/O
              I don't know.

(CONTINUED)

190      CONTINUED:                                              190

The audience groan.

                        PREM
              Oh...

                        LATIKA V/O
              I've never known.

                        PREM
              You really are on your own, now,
              Jamal. Your answer: for twenty
              million rupees.

Jamal shrugs.

                        JAMAL
              A.

                        PREM
              A. Because?

                        JAMAL
              Just...because.

                        PREM
              Apka final jawab?

                        JAMAL
              Yes. Final answer. A. Aramis.

The lights dim, the music crescendoes. A buzz runs around
the audience. Prem pushes the button on his computer.
Stares hard at Jamal.

                        PREM
              Computer-ji A lock kiya-jaye.
              Jamal Malik, Call Centre Assistant
              from Mumbai, for two Crore, twenty
              million rupees, you were asked who
              the Third Musketeer was in the
              novel by Alexandre Dumas. You used
              your final life-line to phone a
              friend. You answered A.
              Aramis.....which is...I have to
              tell you...the correct answer!

Wild applause. Prem jumps up and pulls a bemused Jamal to
his feet, raising his arm in the air. Jamal is smiling,
but disorientated.

                        PREM (CONT'D)
              Ladies and Gentlemen, Jamal Malik,
              Crorepati! What a night!
                        (MORE)

                                                  (CONTINUED)

190     CONTINUED: (2)                                          190

                          PREM (CONT'D)
                We have all been present at the
                making of history, Ladies and
                Gentlemen! Jamal Malik,
                millionaire!

                          JAMAL
                Latika? Latika?

        To ever-increasing roars and applause from the audience,
        Prem escorts Jamal off-stage.


191     INT. ROADSIDE SHACK. NIGHT.                              191

        The line goes dead in Latika's hand. She stares down at
        the phone. The bemused family are still eying her like an
        alien. She smiles at them and goes out. The traffic on
        the road is still grid-locked. She starts walking, faster
        and faster. Then she breaks into a run.


192     INT. JAVED'S SAFE-HOUSE. BATHROOM. NIGHT.                192

        A small tv in the bathroom. Salim smiles.

                          JAVED O/S
                Salim! Teri ma ki chute! Salim!

        Javed is banging on the door. Salim gets up from where he
        has been praying. He climbs into the bath which is full
        of bank notes and lies down amongst the money. He reaches
        across for the pistol and picks it up. Smiles slightly as
        Javed smashes down the door, pulls the trigger and shoots
        Javed. He falls onto the floor, dead. But the Thug right
        behind him shoots Salim in the chest. He lies back in the
        bath, the faintest trace of a smile on his face as he
        stares at the pictures of Jamal on the tv.

                          SALIM
                God is good.

        Salim dies.


193     INT. STUDIO. BACKSTAGE. NIGHT.                           193

        Prem and Jamal are being posed by photographers. A giant-
        sized cheque for twenty million rupees is manhandled onto
        the floor by the Floor Manager and an Assistant amidst
        much cheering and laughter. Jamal is snapped next to a
        scowling Prem. The Inspector appears next to them.

                          INSPECTOR
                Just one more thing left, Sir.


                                                       (CONTINUED)

193     CONTINUED:                                          193

Prem smiles.

                         PREM
          Finally, huh?

                      INSPECTOR
          If you'd like to come with me.

He takes Jamal by the arm, leads him backstage.


194     INT/EXT. POLICE JEEP. NIGHT.                        194

Jamal sits silent in the back seat next to the Inspector
as he drives through the traffic. Then:

                       JAMAL
          Truth alone triumphs? I should
          have known better.

The Inspector stops the jeep. Unlocks the handcuffs.
Holds the back door open for Jamal.

                      INSPECTOR
          Thought you might need a lift,
          Sir.

He nods towards the outside world. Dazed, Jamal gets out.

195     EXT. CHHATRAPATI SHIVAJI TERMINUS. NIGHT.           195

Jamal finds himself gazing up at VT station. Slowly, he
wanders inside. The Inspector takes the contents of the
file and tears them slowly in half. Lets the pieces fall
on the ground. Gets back in the jeep and drives away.


196     OMITTED                                             196


197     INT. CHHATRAPATI SHIVAJI TERMINUS. NIGHT.           197

VT station is awash with the evening commute. Thousands
of people crowd the platforms, jostling the only still
figure who is sitting at the base of the statue of
Frederick Stevens. Jamal. Then there is a gap in the wall
of bodies that swirls around him. Jamal gets to his feet.


                                              (CONTINUED)

                              JAMAL
          Latika?

Then she is gone in the melee again. Only to reappear.

                              LATIKA
          Jamal?

Jamal forces himself through the people. Nothing will
stop him. Latika too is shoving them aside until they are
face-to-face. They stop, look at each other, hold each
other's hands tight. The whole station seems frozen, the
only movement from a thousand bodies being Jamal and
Latika.

                         LATIKA (CONT'D)
          I thought we would meet again only
          in death.

He shakes his head.

                              JAMAL
          I knew you'd be watching.

Jamal puts his hand on Latika's chin, turns her head
gently so that she is facing him. He sees the knife scars
on her cheek for the first time. She tries to turn her
head, but he won't let her. Runs his hand slowly down the
scar. Rests his hand there.

                         JAMAL (CONT'D)
          This is our destiny.

He gently kisses the scarred cheek.

                         JAMAL (CONT'D)
          This is our destiny.

The camera pulls back and back, rising above the station.
The music starts and the frozen station comes alive, two
thousand kurta-clad men and saree-clad women dancing in
and out and on top of the trains, an unbound celebration
of hope and humanity that has at its centre, Jamal and
Latika.

THE END.

# Q & A

## WITH DANNY BOYLE
### BY ROB FELD

*I've heard you speak about using contrasts in films and how they should be jagged and not too smooth. Can you tell me more about that notion and what film is to you?*

**Danny Boyle:** I don't want to make smooth movies. I don't want them to be a reflective experience, I want them to be a voluble experience, where you can't sit back on it or take your eyes off it. You're not always successful doing it, but I try to make films that are, in a way, unavoidable. I want it to press you, and one of the things that helps is the momentum maintained by change, variation, and a jaggedness.

*You mean a visual jaggedness, but also maybe in its narrative, as well?*

**DB:** Yes, the twists it takes, whatever. Sometimes it's based on performance, the surprise of a change. You would think an actor would want to be smooth and make a coherent sense all the way through, but you're constantly challenging actors not to do that. Obviously, you want the character to be coherent, but it doesn't have to be done smoothly. It can actually be made up of many different ingredients of a character's personality and action, so it can surprise you. I try to find that. As you get more experience, one of the things you learn is to try and find that variation in an actor's performance.

But you have to be very careful. For instance, we had a scene where they are looking down on the construction that's happening in the slum. They said, "Look, there's the slum where we used to live." The Western attitude would be, *Wow, look at the change that's happening!* But actually, a kid growing

---

**Rob Feld** interviewed Danny Boyle in New York City, on October 24, 2008. Feld is a screenwriter whose writings on film and interviews with noted filmmakers appear regularly in such publications as the Writers and Directors Guild journals, *Written By* and *DGA Quarterly*, as well as in the Newmarket Press Shooting Script® series.

up in a slum thinks, *Wow, that's where we used to live.* So you have to try and root moments in things that are surprising, rather than things you expect. Roles are set in patterns all the time, and if you can, you want to avoid those patterns in the way people behave.

You hear stories about how annoying some actors can be, but often what they are trying to do is find a different way of playing something very, very obvious, and that's very healthy. Sometimes it needs the obvious, but if the audience is ahead of you and can see it coming, it's not that exciting. Then you certainly don't get that unpredictable momentum I was talking about, of watching something evolve before your eyes that isn't fixed. Film is weird, of course. It is fixed; it's 120 minutes, which are unchangeable. But actually, it doesn't work like that. One of the weirdest things I ever found out about films was that they actually do change, depending on the audience, on where it's played, how full the house is, what time of the day it's playing, what's happened outside the cinema, or moments before in world politics. Different things swim in and out of focus in it. It's so weird and you can contribute to that as a filmmaker, I think, by finding as much variation as possible.

**So it's finding surprises and originality.**

**DB:** But it doesn't have to be just those things. For instance, music. You can score something in a certain way to contradict what you're seeing. There's a great bit where Jamal gets up in the middle of the night and he watches his brother, who is going out to kill someone. You could play that with a great deal of suspense as a very acute moment of discovery about his brother, but actually what the composer did was put this incredible, savage beat track on it. It's like what's going through the guy's head. That's the thinking of it, he's psyching himself. He doesn't just wander around and kill someone, he's got this sense in his head of what he's going to do.

**So, in some sense it's an effort to put the audience in the point of view of the character, subjective as opposed to external and objective?**

**DB:** I would certainly like to do that. I'd like to feel subjective the whole time, if you can be. The classic way of being objective is to have wide shots and let people see the whole scenario, but I like to do it more subjectively, so that you're thrust into the middle of it. You're not going to get the wide relief; but if you do use it, you use it in a punchy way. What you want to do in the short term is make people feel like they're there. It sounds simple, but it's sometimes complicated to achieve.

***You're a very visual director. How do you start finding the visual gram-
mar that puts you in that subjective stance for each specific film, and how did
you talk to your director of photography and designers about this film?***

**DB:** The language for this came from the streets of Mumbai, and the
technicalities of having to work there. It was clear to me early on that the way
I'd worked at home—you get control of a street and re-creating reality in it,
shooting it as many times as you want—was clearly not in the cards in Mumbai.
It wasn't going to be like that. It's too complicated to control and certainly,
in my opinion, too complicated to replicate with any truthfulness. So we
embraced it fully and changed from what we originally set out to do. We
did some tests on film cameras, which I hated, actually. The stuff was really
everything I didn't want the film to be. But that tells you, *Now I know the
way I'm* not *going to do this film.* So we moved to a digital system, which was
actually a prototype with lots of teething problems because it wasn't quite
ready to use, but was wonderful for us because it was very light and flexible.

***The whole film was shot in digital?***

**DB:** About 75 percent of it. Anthony, our DP, was able to hand-hold
the SI-2K cameras. Although they had a gyro on them to stabilize them,
they were still very small and could operate in very small, narrow areas, which
is what you get in the slums. You can capture a bit of the life that's going on
around you without people realizing it and becoming self-conscious.

We also used what we called a "CanonCam," which was a Canon stills
camera, which takes twelve frames a second. If people see a still camera,
they don't think it is recording live action. We'd record stuff like that, as
well as occasionally using the traditional film camera—so it's a mixture of different technologies that we used in the film. Whoever was operating the
camera would have a hard drive strapped to their back, which would record
the images while the camera was in their hand. Anthony would look like a
rather cumbersome tourist from Denmark who was wandering around the
slums, but actually what he was doing was filming.

And it confounded people in Mumbai as well who, if they ever do see a
film camera, it's a big cumbersome thing with a lot of palaver around it. But
this was able to be much more flexible and allowed us to go lots of places
which would be deemed unrealistic for a conventional film crew and equipment. It let us behave with a kind of fluidity, which I thought was in the script;
it's certainly in the city. The whole place is just like water, sloshing everywhere, people and movement and energy, and too much traffic. It's just a
typical, bustling, fast-forward city. And this was a really great way of captur-
ing it. If you're successful, you capture a bit of it. You're never going to get

it all. I had to be dragged away at the end because you're dissatisfied, you don't think you've got enough of it. You're always dissatisfied, and that's a sign that you've bitten off more than you can chew, which is true of a situation like trying to capture Mumbai.

The hyperkinetic chase sequence involving the young Jamal and Salim at the beginning of the film, in particular, was filmed incrementally, built up like a montage over a period of time. Whenever possible, the crew would return to the location and film another section of the chase.

*So, embrace the chaos?*

**DB:** You're forced to, really. You can't deny it, you can't control it, you can't change it. I mean, you can do all those things, but you spend a disproportionate amount of your time and money doing it. And, more important than that, it's not very good when you do. It doesn't feel real; it doesn't feel like the place. When we did some of it we looked at it and thought, *Do we really believe that?* It's like recording live sound there. The live sound is *terrible*, but it is real, and if you do it without the live sound, if you rebuild the sound, it doesn't sound quite so convincing.

*The story has something of an epic quality for me. It covers the full lives of its characters but avoids the pitfalls that many biopics fall into in trying to cover too much time. How did you and Simon think about structuring it to keep the story moving?*

**DB:** A lot is in the script and, as with any good script, even more of it is in the editing. You take stuff out. There was a whole story strand at the end which we eventually went in and very precisely excised. It was a kind of red herring, a MacGuffin kind of thing. And we decided we didn't need it and went for a cleaner narrative. It was already complex in terms of time structure, so we decided to leave that element out. I've never made a film over two hours, and I never want to. I think if you can't do it in two hours, *Come on, guys!* So that discipline helps because if you can't get it all in two hours, you've got to think, *Well, what can we take out?* That helps you because in a weird kind of way, you're the most qualified person to edit the film, but you're also the *least* qualified because you know it too well.

*How do you think about spacing information to keep the audience guessing, posing questions and answering them later?*

**DB:** That's Simon, a lot of that. That's what's wonderful about the adaptation. Unlike the book, which is quite rigid and segmented, he just let everything flow backward and forward so he could give you information way before you needed it. And then if you hung on to it, you felt really intelligent later when it came up again. He would also deny you stuff until way beyond when it seemed relevant, which makes it feel more accidental, that Jamal's good fortune feels earned, rather than just convenient. The danger of a script like this is to have things just feel too convenient. So he set it up very skillfully and was very fluid with time differences, i.e., we didn't really have any because, although things are happening ten years ago and five years ago, there are no indicators, like there's no color coding, there's no white frames to take you back and bring you forward.

Of course, we have three different actors playing the characters at different ages to differentiate time, which allowed us to move fluidly backward and forward. It's not written like that, but it allowed us to do it because it sets up like that. It allowed us in the editing to go backward and forward whenever we wanted, really, almost on a whim. Not a whim, an instinctive feeling to go back in time for that line, rather than wait here for it *now*. Instead of her saying, "My name is Latika," you cut back to where she is seven years old in the rain going, "My name is Latika." We could go back ten years for one line and then come straight back again.

### Dev Patel was a find.

**DB:** It's amazing to look at him now at the press junkets. Meeting him at the hotel now, he is so handsome. They dress him up a little bit but he was a kid, you know? He did four or five auditions and every single audition his mom came. I thought, *How are we going to get rid of his mom?* Serious romantic lead and he's got his mom attached to him. She is a very nice woman, but he couldn't say anything, so it was up to me to separate them.

### What went into your choice to cast him as Jamal?

**DB:** Casting was done in Mumbai, so I met loads of actors there, some very talented young guys. But if you're eighteen or twenty and want to get into Bollywood movies, you've got to be able to get the shirt off. I mean, they stand in the waterfalls in Switzerland and do the song and dance routine, and they've got to be *ripped*. So they were all beefcake, you know, when guys can't put their arms down because they've got too much muscle mass under there? And because they are eighteen, because they are only just beyond kids, their heads are really small. So you've got these tiny little heads with beefcake bodies, and that was wrong for the film.

So my daughter said, "You should see this guy in *Skins*," which is this program we are having in the UK. Dev plays a fairly small comic part in it, but he was very good. So I met him and his mom and he was great. He was very serious about the craft. We did not always agree about stuff and fought a couple of times about things, which is good, because I have a bit of a reputation and he was seventeen. I could see he was quite determined and tough. You want your lead actor to be like that. He did not just do what I said, and that is a really good sign. I'd say, "You've got to smile now. You have got to fucking smile in this section of the script." And he would shake his head, and that is good.

It gets on your nerves at the time, because you are trying to get the thing done and there is so little time, but you want your lead actor to take responsibility for the film and his character; and he had this idea about this character. And I think he was right, the way he did it. He had that sense of himself in the way that Jamal has got a sense of what he wants. Jamal will use this show, not for the money but to get back to Latika. Nothing is going to stop him, whatever it is. That scene when Jamal jumps in the shit; that is his character completely in that scene. Nothing will stand in the way of his dreams and that autograph. And Dev is a bit like that.

**How was it for you to come into a culture and country that weren't your own to tell its story?**

**DB:** I would say you feel a lot of responsibility. You worry about yourself as a Westerner. I did not want to make a film where Westerners go around India. But still you are a Westerner yourself, and I wanted to make it as instinctively and subjectively as possible, so you felt like you were looking at it from the inside. One of the dangers of India is that *wow!* factor, where you go, *Wow! Look at that!* And it feels like you are using it, objectifying it, as some kind of thing to just stare at. They hate that, and people asked us not to do that. We did these film tests at the beginning which felt a bit like that because, for a cameraman, to shoot in India is a dream come true. Photographically it's a place for a coffee table book, so the danger with cinematographers is they go, *Wow, wow, the colors! Wow!* And I did not want that.

I want us to be hurtled into it. I love action, movement. I love action movies, even really bad ones. I *love* them because I think there is something about why films are called *motion pictures*. I really believe that about films. There is a kineticism about them that is wonderful. They should not always be a reflective medium; it does not suit being reflective.

I remember meeting an actor and trying to get him to play a really good part in a film. But he said he wouldn't do it because he dies before the end of the film. I said, *"What?"* And he said, "Listen, nobody in films remembers anybody who has died." And it's absolutely true; what's amazing about films is that you just keep moving. Sure, you may have a sad moment, but then you just move forward. It is all about forward motion, moving forward like that. And so I tried to bring that to it because the society itself feels like that. Bombay feels like it is living in fast forward.

This is kind of an admission, but because the British ruled India until 1948, quite recently in historical terms, you go there and you expect people to remember you. Supposedly up until about twenty years ago it was true, the people used to take note as the white guy went by. *The white man is here*, and all that kind of stuff. But they just do not see you now. They see their society and tiger economy hurtling forward at such a pace that they see themselves as Brazil, America, Russia, China. That is where they see themselves, against these big economies. Either established, like America, or arriving. And you, the British, are an anecdote, a footnote. That is the first thing I felt, very strongly, almost immediately.

And the second thing was that it is just people everywhere. There is nothing to look at other than people. And finally, I suppose, the third thing, which is wonderful for storytelling, is that they do not separate extremes. There are such extremes of wealth, poverty, happiness, sadness, horror, just extraordinary kind of redemptive things and they do not separate them. Everybody lives with everything all the time, and I am sure that is why the storytelling there is very melodramatic. I think we tended to soften the edges in living our lives in the West. We tend to create a comfort zone for ourselves, have separated things like poverty from ourselves, whereas there they sort of sit together much more. So even the Bollywood stars, like Anil Kapoor, who played Prem, feel really connected to the community there. You would meet these people whose hands had been cut off to make them better beggars. And Anil feels a kind of connection with that person unlike the way we view things. Our stars do charity, of course, but it's not like that. They are out the whole time giving them food, and it feels inseparable.

As a place to tell a story, to drive a story through, India was fantastic. Simon said he had a very Dickensian experience writing it. And certainly it was so for me, directing it. The energy of the place, the potential, what was going on; I loved it. I think that comes across in the film. We took about ten crew altogether, and three or four of them did not enjoy it. You could tell. If you go with the right attitude, it is an incredible experience. It changes you forever.

### How did this project come to you, and why choose it?

**DB:** My agent sent me the script and rather lazily said, "It's a film about *Who Wants to Be a Millionaire*." And I thought, "What? They want to make a film about *Who Wants to Be a Millionaire*?" He's always trying to get me to make an American film and I never do. "You won't want to do this, but I am sending it anyway." And then I saw Simon Beaufoy's name on it, and I thought I'd better read at least fifty pages of it, ring him up and say, "You know, thanks, but…." But I was locked ten pages in. You know when you are going to do something. It does not always happen, but sometimes you just know, and you should not wait until you get to the end. Because when you get to the end, all the realities of filmmaking kick in: *How can we cast it? Will we ever be able to raise enough money? Who will distribute it?* But when you're involved in it, you just think, *I've got to make this.*

It's very difficult to describe. It sort of vibrates when you read it. I just read an excellent script the other day by a very skilled screenwriter, and yet I didn't feel that vibration about doing it personally. And the stuff you choose is probably not technically as good as this screenplay. But for some reason, it vibrates in front of you. I remember with *Trainspotting*, when I read the book, the first page, I can virtually quote it verbatim. And I remember reading that first page thinking, *We are going to make this.* You have these instincts.

I remember meeting Freida Pinto to play Latika and thinking, *I will bet that is her.* You don't get it about everybody or everything, but when you do get it and it comes naturally, it just pops. You should always follow that instinct because there is something there that you do not really understand fully, and that is a good thing because you will learn what it is while you are making it. It is funny like that. I cannot explain it anymore than that. But that is the truth; it is not more complex than that or more cunning than that, or anything.

### What did you get from the experience of India?

**DB:** You realize, it's your own eyes you open. You are not there to teach anybody anything. You are there to learn about yourself, and you do, and how extraordinary the world is and these people are. The people who live in these slums are extraordinary people. So generous, so resourceful. I want it to be something that they would like. I hope if they ever see it on a pirate copy somewhere that they think, *Yeah, that is okay.*

### How did you develop the aesthetic of the film out of Beaufoy's script?

**DB:** Well, a lot of it is the script. He did an amazing job. The book is twelve or fourteen chapters, and each chapter is a question and answer, question and answer. It's like a series of short stories, and it would never have worked as a film like that. There is no real coherence. What Simon did was this very clever thing where he fed the material in early and spread out the information, so sometimes you got the answer way before the question was even asked and sometimes you did not, you had to wait. And it makes you feel very intelligent reading; I always love that. It is a very good instance of showing what it is to adapt a novel. You could read the novel and not see how he has done it at all.

So you feel it as you read and you start to see it. Then we went and visited India, and as soon as we were there, I thought, *Oh, I am going to do this.* Just to walk through areas of Bombay—there is nothing to look at really, no architecture, just people. You have got to like people.

### What was the production experience like in that environment?

**DB:** What matters more than anything is your attitude. You have to go in with the right attitude. You cannot control the process, and directors are really about control. One of the things you are trying to do all the time is control experience and repeat it, capture it, but you cannot do that in India. It is just irrelevant. You will just drive yourself mad. It's like Canute and the sea, trying to stop the sea, let's just forget it. You've got to plunge in and just go with it. It's a lot of risk taking because you aren't certain that you're getting shots. You have to wait until you get into the cutting room. But, actually, what you find is that you got much greater results than you thought you would ever have.

### You have a co-director on this film, Loveleen Tandan.

**DB:** She was the casting director, did an amazing job. I realized when I was working with her that I needed her on the set every day. She wants to be a director, as well, and she can do it. And that was not just for the kids who only spoke Hindi, it was for everything, really. And I could test things against her, cultural elements and stuff like that; also when I knew I wanted to make a mistake and do something inaccurately, because you do do that—films have their own justice and logic, which is not applicable to the country, necessarily. She was someone I could bounce off, who I trusted, and she was also able to tell me the truth.

One of the problems with being a director is that people often just say yes. If you ask a question, they just go *yes*, and confirm you are right the whole time. Whereas, in fact, you are not. And you find out later to your cost, you know. So she would tell me the truth about how something might happen, no matter how inconvenient it was. If it stops filming it is very inconvenient, but she would tell me the truth and that is really important. I think you have to surround yourself with the right people who you trust and who trust you, but who don't respect you too much so they won't tell you when you're wrong.

And then I sent her off to do the second unit, which had been shooting very badly. And the stuff that came back was fantastic. So we called her co-director because she deserves it. The first assistant director was this guy called Raj Acharya; he runs the floor, a doubly crucial job when you're working out of your own culture. And the guy who did the live sound, Resul Pookutty. Without those three people, it would not have been the film it is at all. They were a very special support system for me. I have to feel at home, you know?

**The tone of the film runs the gamut. How did you think about balancing it?**

**DB:** You don't think like that when you are making films. I don't, anyway. I don't think, *Oh God, this is so tough. How is it ever going to fit with the happy bit here?* There's the blinding of the kid, which is one feeling, and the jump in the shit is another. And the kiss at the end is another. You are trying to get as intense an experience as possible. And then if they do not go together, you would probably never see the film because they'd kill it. It's an intuitive sense, and the writer works like that, as well. And the truth is, I love variation, and that suits India because there are such inseparable extremes going on the whole time. I love that sense of hitting a different note in a film. It's one of the reasons I love using music so much. You can often have the tone of a film just too similar or flat, and you can just pop it with music and it suddenly feels like a different film. It is one of the wonderful ways music works. There are lots of ways you can work on it without really intellectualizing it, as such. It's weird doing these kinds of conversations because you become aware of things like that, and I always worry I'll carry this conversation into the next film, but you do not. You have a kind of amnesia sense. You also have amnesia about the realities of filmmaking and how difficult it is sometimes. You never consider that.

**Were there films you watched in preparation for making Slumdog?**

**DB:** Not so much on this film. But I did do a lot of research. The only book you need to read is *Maximum City,* by Suketu Mehta. It is just a drop-dead book. I read that all the time, and half the time I thought I was adapting that, not *Q&A,* the book we actually meant to be adapting.

When I got to India, there were three films I had never heard of that I did watch, and they do influence the film in some way. And one is called *Satya,* which is as good a film as I have seen. It is written by and stars our fat police constable, the guy who tortures him, Saurabh Shukla. He is an amazing writer and terrific character actor. There was another film called *Company,* which is a very good film about gangsters in Bombay. And another film called *Black Friday,* which is about the bombings in Mumbai, made by a young guy called Anurag Kashyap. It is a fantastic film as well. They were inspirations while we were making it.

*How did you get the performances out of these kids with whom you couldn't communicate without a translator?*

**DB:** Performances are not difficult because they are really good actors. I mean, the kids there love acting. They'll ask if you want this or that look from this or that film. And you go, *I do not want any of that.* But once you get them to understand the world that they are in, you just want a kind of realism, they are terrific. They do not feel a separation between themselves and film. It's so natural for film to be a part of life for them. Everybody has been to the cinema. Even seven-year-olds have seen lots and can talk to you about stuff. But finding them was really due to Loveleen.

Initially the film was written completely in English, but when we got there and started seeing children who speak a bit of English, it didn't work because they were not that deft with English at seven, eight. They get better when they get into their teens. So Loveleen said, "Listen, you should really do it in Hindi." I, of course, thought, *Oh my God, what's Warner Brothers going to say if I do that?* So she adapted the dialogue and as soon as she did it, the kids suddenly came to life. It felt so real suddenly. So I did ring Warner Brothers and said, "We're going to do the first third in Hindi with English subtitles." They just thought I was losing my mind, like I was Colonel Kurtz and I was going to come back with a five-hour film about meditation or yoga or something. But we tried to make the subtitles vibrant and different, not just read them at the bottom of the screen, but pop around the screen and be read like a comic book. If somebody speaks, we put it on a level with their eye line and things like that, so when you look on the screen it is easy to take in.

*It must have been tricky to find a connection between three different sets of actors.*

**DB:** It was, because if you found one person, you had to be wary because you might not find someone else who looked like them at all. I mean, you want them to look a bit like each other, but mostly you just hope that the audience goes with it. If you did it with enough confidence, they just accept. It is not the same person, it is just really actors, but there is a feeling of a connection between them. We had them all together in rehearsal, so they all got to look at each other. I tried to get them to copy each other's mannerisms and to make the whole thing feel coherent.

I'll say America is to blame for this: You see these programs on TV where twenty-nine-year-old girls are playing fourteen-year-olds. And you say, Give me a break. That is just ridiculous." So I had always wanted to do it properly, so that if you had a fourteen-year-old and a twenty-nine-year-old, you play them with different people and just go with the idea that they're same person.

*You weren't mimicking Bollywood films, but you did end with a dance.*

**DB:** In India it is song and dance in the movies and in life. The little kids would get up and do little bits of dances from films for me. Everybody can, so it is all around you the whole time. I lived and worked there for eight months. If you live and work in Bombay, you cannot leave without a dance. You cannot. It would be like making a film about America without a motorcar. It would be wrong and so fake not to do it, like we had not been there or had made the film at arm's length or something. So the key thing was whether we should put it inside the film, as one of the questions linked to a question, for example (we thought there would be a clue in a song and dance that would maybe answer a question, but it did not work out that way). Or whether we put it at the end of the film, as it is right now. So we decided to put it at the end of the film and celebrate that love. It is absolutely genuine. Their love of movies, dancing, and song is something to be absolutely celebrated.

*The film you did just prior to this one,* **Sunshine,** *was shot entirely on a soundstage, right? Was the ability to be on location part of the appeal of* **Slumdog?**

**DB:** It certainly felt like a chance to do something so different. And there is not more of a contrast to outer space than Mumbai. And I love that change because *Sunshine* took too long, and it was too isolated an experience making it. You were cut off from people. It was also so meticulous, the detail. You cannot worry about that in India. Space movies are all about control, but in India you can't control things. You just waste your budget trying to control anything. And if you respect it, you get back magnificent benefits that sometimes you are aware of when they're happening.

For example, they make over a thousand movies a year in Mumbai alone. In the West, even really famous actors are basically out of work most of the time, so when you do your film, you don't quite have their undivided attention, but you've got them. But in India, they are doing three, four, five films all at the same time. Some of them they are shooting at night, and then they turn up for yours in the daytime. And then they go back on the night shoot. And some of them cannot turn up at all. They say, "I cannot come next week." And you go, "What? We are doing the big scenes next week!" And he'll say, "Oh, I know. I can come the week after, though." And your instinct is to go, *God!* And you cannot. You've just got to trust your first assistant director, who knows the way it works. He has all these mobile phones in front of him, to all these other first assistant directors and all these other films. And they are doing deals and money is changing hands and deals are being done and favors are called in and dispensed. And finally you get the scene done and it is very good. And the other film gets their scene done as well, and somehow it works.

# CAST AND CREW CREDITS

A FOX SEARCHLIGHT PICTURES
WARNER BROS. PICTURES
CELADOR FILMS
FILM4 Presentation
A CELADOR FILMS Production
A DANNY BOYLE Film

## SLUMDOG MILLIONAIRE

DEV PATEL   FREIDA PINTO   MADHUR MITTAL   ANIL KAPOOR   IRRFAN KHAN

| | | |
|---|---|---|
| Directed by<br>DANNY BOYLE | Director of Photography<br>ANTHONY DOD MANTEL BSC DFF | Music Composed and Produced by<br>A. R. RAHMAN |
| Co-Director (India)<br>LOVELEEN TANDAN | Production Designer<br>MARK DIGBY | Costume Designer<br>SUTTIRAT ANNE LARLARB |
| Screenplay by<br>SIMON BEAUFOY | Editor<br>CHRIS DICKENS | Sound Designer<br>GLENN FREEMANTLE |
| Produced by<br>CHRISTIAN COLSON | Co-Producer<br>PAUL RITCHIE | Sound Mixer<br>RESUL POOKUTTY |
| Based on the Novel "Q&A"By<br>VIKAS SWARUP | Line Producer<br>TABREZ NOORANI | Make Up & Hair Design<br>NATASHA NISCHOL &<br>VIRGINIA HOLMES |
| Executive Producers<br>PAUL SMITH, TESSA ROSS | Co-Executive Producers<br>FRANÇOIS IVERNEL<br>CAMERON McCRACKEN | Casting by<br>LOVELEEN TANDAN<br>GAIL STEVENS CDG |

## CAST
### (In order of appearance)

Older Jamal . . . . . . . . . . DEV PATEL
Sergeant Srinivas . . . SAURABH SHUKLA
Prem. . . . . . . . . . . . ANIL KAPOOR
Director. . . . . . . . . . . RAJ ZUTSHI
Vision Mixer . . . . . . JENEVA TALWAR
Older Latika. . . . . . . . FREIDA PINTO
Police Inspector . . . . . . IRRFAN KHAN
Youngest Salim
. . AZHARUDDIN MOHAMMED ISMAIL
Youngest Jamal
. . . . . AYUSH MAHESH KHEDEKAR
Airport Security Guards . HIRA BANJARA
. . . . . . . . . . . . . . SHEIKH WALI
Javed. . . . . . MAHESH MANJREKAR
Jamal's Mother
. . . . . . . . SANCHITA CHOUDHARY
Mr Nanda . . . . . HIMANSHU TYAGI
Prakash . . . . . . . . SHARIB HASHMI
Slum Man . . VIRENDRA CHATTERJEE
Amitabh Bachchan . . . . FEROZE KHAN
Mr Chi . . . . . . . SUNIL AGGARWAL

Man on Fire
. . . . . VIRENDER KUMAR GHARU
Blue Boy. . . . . . . . DEVESH RAWAL
Youngest Latika. . . . . . . RUBINA ALI
Maman . . . . . . . . . ANKUR VIKAL
Punnoose . . . . . . . . . . . . TIGER
Young Arvind. . . . . CHIRAG PARMAR
Baby . . . . . . . . . NAZNEEN SHAIKH
Latika's Friend . . . . FARZANA ANSARI
Old Villager . . . . . . ANUPAM SHYAM
Ticket Collector . . . . . SALIM CHAUS
Family in Train . SINGH SHERA FAMILY
  HARINDER KAUR, NARENDRA SINGH
Middle Jamal
. . . . . . TANAY HEMANT CHHEDA
Middle Salim
. . . . ASHUTOSH LOBO GAJIWALA
Taj Mahal Guide . . . . SATYA MUDGAL
Ada. . . . . . . . . . JANET DE VIGNE
Peter . . . . . . . . WILLIAM RELTON
Clark . . . . . . . . . DAVID GILLIAM
Adele . . . . . . . . MIA INDERBITZIN
Driver . . . . . . . . . KINDER SINGH

Opera Singers . CHRISTINE MATOVICH SINGH, THOMAS LEHMKUHL
Older Arvind . . . . . . SIDDESH PATIL
Women at Brothel . . . . NAJMA SHAIKH, SAEEDA SHAIKH, ALKA SATPUTE, TABASSUM KHAN
Middle Latika . . TANVI GANESH LONKAR
Dance Teacher . . . SITARAM PANCHAL
Hotel Security Guard . . . NIGEL CAESAR
Javed's Goons . . . AJIT PANDEY, KEDAR THAPAR, AMIT LEONARD, RAJESH KUMAR, SAGAR GHOPALKAR, PRADEEP SOLANKI, HAMID SHEIKH, DHEERAJ WAGHELA
Call Centre Instructor . . SHRUTI S SETH
Bardi . . . . . . . . . . . . ARFI LAMBA
Nasreen . . . . . . . . . . TAIRA COLAH
Call Centre Trainee . . . . VARUN BAGRI
Dave . . . . . . . . . ANKUR TEWARI
Operator . . . . . . . . ANJUM SHARMA
Mrs MacKintosh . . . . JANET DE VIGNE
Older Salim . . . . . . MADHUR MITTAL
Autorickshaw Drivers . . . . . SARFARAZ KHAN, SYED HUSSAIN, UMER KHAN
Javed's House Doorkeeper
. . . . . . . . . . . . . . . IMRAN HASNEE
KBC Contestant . . HOMAI BILLIMORIA
Cricket Commentator . . UDAYAN BAIJAL
Floor Manager . . . . . SANDEEP KAUL
Double for Irrfan Khan . . RUFEE AHMED
TV Reporter . . . . . . RHEA LAWYER
Dancers at Javed's Safehouse . . . . DEEPALI DALVI, ANISHA NAGAR, FARAH SHAIKH, MAMTA SHARMA, NEHA M KHATARAWALLA
Newsreaders . . TANYA SINGH, ANAND TIWARI, FAEZEH JALALI, MEGHANA JHALANI, RUPALI MEHRA, ANJU SINGH
Call Centre Manager
. . . . . . . . . . SAURABH AGARWAL

## CREW

First Assistant Director . . . RAJ ACHARYA
Production Supervisor . PRAVESH SAHNI
Unit Production Manager
. . . . . . . . . . . . . SANJAY KUMAR
Production Manager (Agra)
. . . . . . . . . . . . . RAJEEV MEHRA
Production Manager (UK)
. . . . . . . . . . . . JENNIFER WYNNE
Production Services India
. . INDIA TAKE ONE PRODUCTIONS

Post Production Supervisor
. . . . . . . . . . . . . LUCIE GRAVES
First Assistant Editor
. . . . . . . CATRIONA RICHARDSON
Second Assistant Director . . AVANI BATRA
Second Second Assistant Director
. . . . . . . . . SONIA NEMAWARKAR
Third Assistant Director
. . . . . YUGANDHAR S. NARVEKAR
Action Director . . . . . SHAM KAUSHAL
First Assistant Camera . TELFER BARNES, DEVENDRA THAKKAR, G MONIC KUMAR
Second Assistant Camera . . . . . . SATISH VENKATARAMANA, B DURGA KISHORE KUMAR, UDITA BHARGAVA
B Camera Operator . . . STEFAN CIUPEK
First Assistant Digital Camera
. . . . . . . . . . . . . . VISHAL JAIN
Steadicam Operator
. . . . . . . . . . . SUNIEL KHANDPUR
Steadicam Assistants . . . . . SALIM KHAN, VICKY KHANDPUR
Camera Attendants . PRADIPTA KUMAR PRADHAN, RISHIRAJ GARG, MANISH M GHADGE
VTR Operator . . . HEMCHANDRA RAI
Camera Loader . TANAJI S. KSHIRSAGAR
VTR Assistant
. . . RASHIKANT MAHESH RAJPURE
Continuity Supervisors . HASSAN KUTTY 1957-2008, NUVENDRA SINGH "NIKI"
Script Editor . . . . . JULIETTE HOWELL
Hindi Dialogue Translation
. . . . . . . . . . . LOVELEEN TANDAN
Sound Associates . . SHALINI AGARWAL. AMRIT PRITAM DUTTA
Boom Operator . . . GHULAM HUSSAIN
Cableman . . MUSTAQ SHAIKH YUNUS
Assistant Stunt
. . . "PAMMA" PRAMJEET DHILLION
Car Rig . . . MEHBOOB G MOHAMED
Financial Controller . . . DEBBIE MOORE
Production Accountant
. . . . . . . . PARESH NATH BEHERA
Accountants . . . . . PARDEEP KHANNA, DEEPAK JAITELY
Book Keeper . . . . . . AMIT RASTOGI
Production Co-ordinator (Delhi)
. . . . . . . . . . . . SUPRIYA BAGGA
Production Co-ordinator (Mumbai)
. . . . . . . . . . . . . AARTI BHATIA
Tech. Consultant (Production/Digital Camera) . . . . . . . TUSHAAR MEHRA

Production Co-ordinator (Equipment)
. . . . . . . . . . . . . . . RAKESH SINGH
Product Placement & Clearances
. . . . . . . . . . . . . . . AMAR BUTALA
Hotel & Travel Agency Co-ordinator
. . . . . . . . . . . . PRADEEP ARORA
Transport Assistant . . SAURABH SUMAN
Production Assistants . . . ADNAN SHAH,
KARAM PATEL
Director's Assistant . . . . MAXIMA BASU
Assistant to Danny Boyle (UK)
. . . . . . . . . . . . GAIA ELKINGTON
Key Set PA . . . . . CHIRAG NIHALANI
Set PAs . . . . MOHD. SHAREEFUDDIN,
ROHIT GABA
Film Courier & Post Production Runner
. . . . . . . . . . . . . . MONAL DUTIA
Office Boy . . . . . . . . RAHIM SHEIKH
Production Runners. ABBAS ALI SHAIKH,
PRITHVIRAJ SAHOO, GANESH SINGH
BIST, KHIRESWOR DAS, VISHAL
SINGH
Spot Boys . . . . MOHD. SALIM SHAIKH,
KUNJ BIHARI ASSATTI, SHEKHAR
DEVADIGA, SAYYED
TAFAZZUL HUSSAIN
Location Manager . . . . . . NAVIT DUTT
Assistant Location Manager
. . . . . . . . . . RAHUL KHANDARE
Location Assistant
. . . . . MAHENDRA KUMAR SINGH
Railway Co-ordinator
. . . . . . . . . . PRAKASH AGARWAL
Railway Assistant. . . . . . . . . SACHIN
Base Manager. . . SANJAY CHATURVEDI
Location Manager (Agra)
. . . . . . . . . . . . . KAUSHIK GUHA
Assistant Location Manager (Agra)
. . . . . . . . . . . . KULDEEP SINGH
Costumer Designer (India)
. . . . . . . . . RIYAZALI MERCHANT
Wardrobe Supervisor
. . . . . . . . . ONAIZA MOOSABHOY
Wardrobe Assistant
. . . . . . . . . BHARAT MANDEKAR
Assistant Wardrobe Supervisor
. . . . . . . . . MANSINGH SHAKYA
Dressman . . . . . . . JAKIR HOSSAIN,
SACHIN RAHATE
Tailor . . . . . DEVAPUTHRA MADRI
Make-up Assistants . . KAMLESH SHINDE,
ABHISHEK AMANE
Hair Assistants . . . HOMAI BILLIMORIA,
LEENA SANIL

Special Effects Supervisor (India)
. . . . . . . . . SHIVANANDA MOHILI
Digital Media Management
. . . . . . . . . GYANENDRA PRATAP
Art Director . . . . ABHISHEK REDKAR
Art Department Supervisor
. . . . . . . . . . . RAVI SRIVASTAVA
Stand-by Art Director . . . ARWEL EVANS
Assistant Art Directors . . . . . MANOJ N
BHOYAR, WAHID SHAIKH
Art Department Assistant
. . . . . . . . . . . SRINIVAS KONDA
Graphic Designers . . PRAVEEN KUMAR
HENDWAY, SUSHIL KUMAR GIRI
Storyboard Artist
. . . . . . . BRENDAN HOUGHTON
Set Decorator . . . . . . MICHELLE DAY
On Set Dressers . . . . ADITYA KANWAR,
SEEMA KASHYAP
Prop Masters . . AVISHEK BOSE, SACHIN
DABHADE, RAVINDRA JOSHI, RAJ
PATIL
Production Buyer . . . . . AMIT TOMAR
Stand-by Props . . . . . . SWAPNALI DAS
Additional Prop & Set Labour
. . . . . . . . DHARMENDRA YADAV
Construction Head . . . . . SATISH NAIR
Assistant Construction
. . . . . . . . . . VISHAL SRIVASTAVA
Key Grip . . . . . . . . . ARJUN BHURJI
Best Boy . . . BIDHAN BIPUL CHANDA
Grip . . . . . . . . . IKRAM MOHAMAD
Gaffer . . . . . . . . . THOMAS NEIVELT
Gaffer (India) . . . MULCHAND DEDHIA
Light Boys . ANESH MAHADIC, NIZAM
KHAN, PRAVEEN BHUWAAD, ABID
ALI, JAMIL AHMED, VINAYAK PARAB,
SURESH YADAV, MAHESH RATATE
Generator Operators
. . . SADRUDDIN MISTRY, FAROQUE
KHAN, SWAPNESH PRADHAN
Transport Manager . . . BHAWANI SINGH
Transport Captain . . . . . . RAJU ATKAR
Transport Assistant . . SAURABH SUMAN
Casting Associate (UK)
. . . . . KELLY VALENTINE HENDRY
Casting Assistant (UK) . . . . . TOM REED
Casting Assistants (India) . RHEA LAWYER
SWAPNIL KORE, NEHA SINGH
Extras Supplied by . . . . PAPPU LEKHRAJ
Catering . . . . . TIAN RESTAURANT
A Catering Managers . JAIDAVE PANDA &
KALIM SHEIKH

Health & Safety Advisor
. . . . . . . . . DAVID KING TAYLOR
Unit Doctor . . . . DR. PANKAJ PANDYA
UK Publicist . . . . . . . IAN THOMSON
Unit Publicist (India) . . NILUFER QURESHI
Still Photographer . . . . ISHIKA MOHAN
Additional Photographers
. . KERRY MONDINE, KEVIN NUNES
"Making Of" Footage Shot by . SREEJITH
VFX Editor/Second Assistant Editor
. . . . . . . . . . . . . TOM KEMPLEN
Assembly Editors . VIVEK PRATAP, CELIA
HAINING, ANURADHA SINGH
Assistant Editors . . . . . UDAYAN BAIJAL,
SHIJOY PRABHAKARAN
Supervising Sound Editor/Sound Designers
. GLENN FREEMANTLE, TOM SAYERS
Sound Effects Editor . . . . BEN BARKER
Music Editor/Sound Effects Editor
. . . . . . . . . . . . . . . NIV ADIRI
Supervising Dialogue Editor
. . . . . . . . . . GILLIAN DODDERS
Dialogue Editor . . . . . LEE HERRICK
Foley Editor . . . . . . . HUGO ADAMS
Assistant Sound Editor
. . . . . . . . DANNY FREEMANTLE
Sound Design & Post Production
. . . . . . . . . . . . . . . SOUND 24
ADR Boom . . . . . HAROON SHEIKH
ADR Assistant
. . . . . . RAHUL DILIP KUNKERKA
Additional Sound Recording
. . . . . . . . . VIVEK SACHIDANAND
ADR Mixer . . . . . . . . PAUL CARR
ADR Recorded at
. . GOLDCREST POST PRODUCTION
Foley Recordist . . . . ADAM MENDEZ
Foley Artists . . . . . . . . . JACK STEW,
ANDREA KING, ANDI DERRICK,
PETER BURGIS
Foley Recorded at
. ANVIL POST PRODUCTION, London
Re-recording Mixers . . . . . . IAN TAPP,
RICHARD PRYKE
Assistant Re-recording Mixer
. . . . . . . . . . . ADAM SCRIVENER
Re-recorded at . . PINEWOOD STUDIOS
2nd Unit
Director of Photography . MRINAL DESAI
Co-ordinator . . . . . . DIGVIJAY PUROHIT
First Assistant Director
. . . . . . . . . ROHIT VED PRAKASH
Second Assistant Director . TANYA SINGH
Sound Recordist . . . . . . DARA SINGH

Boom Operator . . . . SAMEER KHAN
Second Assistant Cameraman
. . . . . B DURGA KISHORE KUMAR
Key Grip . . . DHARMENDRA BHURJI
Additional Key Grip . . . INDER BHURJI
Make-up & Hair
. . . . . . . XAVIER PETER D'SOUZA
PA . . . . . . . . . . . KAPIL SHAH
Spot Boy . . . . PARMESHWAR ANNA
Ooty Facilitation . . . . . . T.M.RAFIQUE
Spot Boy (Ooty) . . . . . . . . . SURESH
Rajasthan Facilitation . . . . . ALAM BHAI
Post Production Co-ordinator
. . . . ALEXANDRA MONTGOMERY
Post Production Consultancy
. . JEANETTE HALEY, J&E POST PROD.
Main & End Titles Design by
. . . . . . . . . . MATT CURTIS, AP
Visual Effects by . . . CIS LONDON LTD.
VFX Supervisor . . . . ADAM GASCOYNE
VFX Executive Producer
. . . . . . . . . . ROMA O'CONNOR
Production Manager . . . . . NICK DREW
VFX Producer . . . . . BECKY ROBERTS
VFX Editor . . . . . COLLETTE NUNES
Lead Compositor
. . . . . . . . . HUGH MACDONALD
Compositors . . . PADDY EASON, DAVID
EMENY, SIMON HUGHES, DAVID
WAHLBERG
Digital Film Mastering by . THE MOVING
PICTURE COMPANY
DI Supervisors . . MATTHEW BRISTOWE
BEGOÑA LOPEZ
Colourist . . . . JEAN-CLEMENT SORET
Senior Online Film Editor
. . . . . . . . . RICHARD ETCHELLS
Online Film Editors . . . . . . . PATRICK
WINTERSGILL, JAIME LEONARD,
JAMES CUNDILL
Imaging . . . MARTIN PARSONS, JOHN
FRITH, STEPHANE CATTAN
Software Support . . . . LOUIS MUSTILL,
MARK STREATFIELD, MATTHEW
HANGAR
Music Recorded at
AM STUDIOS, PANCHATHAN
RECORD INN, KM MUSIQ STUDIO
& NIRVANA STUDIO (Mumbai)
Sitar . . . . . . . . . . . . . ASAD
Guitar . . . . . . . . . . RAASHID ALI
Percussion . . . . . . . . RAJA, KUMAR
Vocal Supervision & Music Assistant
. . . . . . . . . . SRINIVASA MURTY

Additional Programming by
. . . . . DEEPAK, CHETAN, VIVIANE
Sound Engineers . . . . . . . H SRIDHAR,
VIVIANE, ADITYA MODI
Co-ordination . . . . . . . . NOEL JAMES,
FAIZZUDDIN, SAMIDURAI
Original Score Mixed by
. ANDY RICHARDS at OUT OF EDEN
Music Associate . . SIMON MORTIMER,
UNIVERSAL MUSIC PUBLISHING LTD.
Legal Services . . . . . . . . . OLSWANG
Music Legal Services . NORA MULLALLY
Script Clearances (UK) . . TONIA COHEN
Insurance Services
. . . TOTALLY ENTERTAINMENT LTD.
Completion Guarantors . . FILM FINANCES
Production Auditors . . . . . . . SHIPLEYS
Mr Kapoor's Costume Provided by
. . . . . REID & TAYLOR INDIA LTD.
Camera Equipment . . . . . ARRI MEDIA
Lighting Consumables . . . . . PANALUX
Film Stock . . . . . . . FUJIFILM UK LTD.
Indian Laboratory . . . . . . . . . KODAK
Telecine Services . . . . . . . . . PIXION
UK Laboratory . . . . . TECHNICOLOR
Laboratory Contact . . . KEITH BRYANT
Editing Equipment . . . . . . GEARBOX
(SOUND AND VISION) LTD, SMART DV
Negative Management . . PROFESSIONAL
NEGATIVE CUTTING
Shipping . . . . GPM FREIGHT SYSTEMS
DHL GLOBAL FORWARDING (UK)
LTD.
UK Unit Cars . CINEFILM CARS, JAMES
LUCK CARS
Post Production Script . . . . . . . FATTS
Who Wants To Be A Millionaire? - India
Producers
SYNERGY ADLABS MEDIA LTD.
Producers . . SIDDHARTHA BASU, ANITA
KAUL BASU, KARUN PRABHKARAN
Director . . . . . . . . . NEERAJ DATTA
Assistant Directors . . SAI SAGA PATNAIK
KEVIN D'SOUZA
Head of Production . . . ANAND SINGH
Production Managers . . . GAGAN DIXIT
AJAZ MISTRY
Directors of Photography . . . . . . AJAY
NORONHA, FAUZAN SHEIKH
Vision Mixer . . . . . . . GAGAN DEEP
Floor Manager . . . . . SANDEEP KAUL
Teleprompter Operator
. . . . . . SHIV PRASAD KANNAUJIA
Video Equipment . . . . . . A S VISION

Lights . . . . . . STAGE GEAR, LITECH
Software/Hardware . . . . . . . EYESOFT
Who Wants To Be A Millionaire? Set Built
by . . . NITIN CHANDRAKANT DESAI
For Celador Films
Associate Producer . IVANA MACKINNON
Production Executive
. . . . . . . . DIARMUID McKEOWN
Head of Finance . . . . MARK JOHNSON
Assistant to Christian Colson & Paul Smith
. . . . . . . . . . . . LAURA JAMES
For Film4
Head of Development
. . . . . . . . . KATHERINE BUTLER
Development Editor . . . SAM LAVENDER
Head of Business Affairs . PAUL GRINDEY
Legal and Business Affairs
. . . . . . . . . . . RAJINDER SHAH
Head of Production . . TRACEY JOSEPHS
Production Manager
. . . . . . . . GERARDINE O'FLYNN
Head of Commercial Development
. . . . . . . . . . SUE BRUCE-SMITH
For Pathé
Business Affairs . . PIERRE DU PLESSIS &
GEORGE PANK
Finance . . . . . . . . JAMES CLARKE
Physical Production
. . . . . . . . . CAROLINE HEWITT
Technical . . . . . . . . . . . LEE BYE
International Sales . . MIKE RUNAGALL &
MURIEL SAUZAY

O...SAYA
Performed by A R Rahman & M.I.A.
Music & Lyrics by A R Rahman & M.I.A.
Produced by A R Rahman
Published by K M Musiq Ltd./Imagem Music

M.I.A. PAPER PLANES (DFA REMIX)
Written by
Strummer/Jones/Simonon/Headon/
Arulpragasam/Pentz
Published by Imagem Music/Hollertronix
Domino Publishing Company Ltd.
Universal Music Publishing Ltd./Nineden
Ltd.
Courtesy of XL Recordings Ltd. and
Interscope
Under licence from Universal Music
Operations Ltd.

RANGA-RANGA
Sung by Alka & Ila Arun

Lyrics by Raqueeb. Music by A R Rahman
Published by K M Musiq Ltd.

LIQUID DANCE
Sung by Sriram
Music by A R Rahman
Published by K M Musiq Ltd.

AAJ KI RAAT
Music by Shankar Ehsaan Loy.
Lyrics by Javed Akhtar
Performed by Sonu Nigam, Mahalaxmi Lyer
& Alisha Chinoi
Published by and courtesy of
Super Cassettes Industries Limited (T-Series)

M.I.A. PAPER PLANES
Written by
Strummer/Jones/Simonon/Headon/
Arulpragasam/Pentz
Published by Imagem Music/Hollertronix
Domino Publishing Company Ltd.
Universal Music Publishing Ltd./Nineden
Ltd.
Courtesy of XL Recordings Ltd. and
Interscope
Under licence from Universal Music
Operations Ltd.

GLUCK: NO.43 (AIR)
(ORPHÉE ET EURYDICE)
Performed by Orchestre des Concerts
Lamoureux
with Hans Rosbaud & Léopold Simoneau
Courtesy of Decca Music Group
Under Licence from Universal Music
Operations Ltd.

GANGSTER BLUES....
Sung by Blaaze & Tanvi
Lyrics by Blaaze. Music by A R Rahman
Published by K M Musiq Ltd.

SEARCH FOR LATIKA
Sung by Susanne
Music & Lyrics by A R Rahman
Published by K M Musiq Ltd.

JAIHO.....
Sung by Sukvinder Singh, Vijay Prakash,
Tanvi
Lyrics by Gulzar. Music by A R Rahman
Published by K M Musiq Ltd.

"WHO WANTS TO BE A
MILLIONAIRE?"
Original Music written by Keith Strachan
and Matthew Strachan
Published by Lusam Music Ltd.

All Rights in "Who Wants To Be A
Millionaire?" are the exclusive property of
2waytraffic,
a Sony Pictures Entertainment Company and
are Reproduced by Kind Permission

Radio Times Magazine Courtesy of BBC
Worldwide
Jessie Wallace as 'Kat Slater' Photo of BBC
'Apne Mere Apne' Clip Courtesy of Mr
Hemant Seth, Behind the Scene
'Reid and Taylor Dress Code' Commercial
Courtesy of Reid and Taylor India Ltd.
'Belmonte: Academy of Style' & 'Belmonte:
Party' Commercials
Courtesy of S Kumars Nationwide Ltd.
(SKNL)
'Future Cup Series India v/s South Africa'
Clip Courtesy of The Board of Control for
Cricket In India
'Lajja' 'Ram Balraam' & 'Chori Chori
Chupke Chupke' Clips
Courtesy of Mr Bharat Shah, Mega
Bollywood Pvt Ltd.
'Fanaa Fanaa' Clip Courtesy of Venus
Records & Tapes Pvt. Ltd. India

The Producers Would Like to Thank
SARAH KING, RICHARD CONWAY,
JESSIE WALLACE
THE HINDUJA GROUP and KETAN
DESAI & MKD FILMS
for the use of the Amtiabh Bachchan Film
Clips
MR & MRS NITIN KASLIWAL of REID
AND TAYLOR INDIA LTD.
ZEE NEWS LTD., THE TIMES GROUP,
ETV NETWORK, JAIN TELEVISION
GLOBAL BROADCAST NEWS
LTD./THE NETWORK 18, BROADCAST
INITIATIVE LTD.

The Producers Would Also Like to Thank
THE GOVERNMENT OF INDIA, MIN-
ISTRY OF INFORMATION &
BROADCASTING
ARCHAEOLOGICAL SURVEY OF
INDIA

Filmed Entirely on Location in India and at
Big ND Studio in Karjat

The characters, businesses and events portrayed in the film are entirely fictitious.
Any resemblance between them and actual individuals, businesses or events is coincidental, not intended and should not be inferred.
This motion picture is protected under the laws of the United Kingdom and other countries and its unauthorised duplication, distribution or exhibition may result in civil liability and criminal prosecution.

# ABOUT THE FILMMAKERS

**SIMON BEAUFOY (Writer)**

Simon Beaufoy trained at Bournemouth College of Art and Design as a documentary director, then took to writing. His screenwriting credits include *The Full Monty, Among Giants, The Darkest Light, Yasmin,* and *This Is Not a Love Song.* Filming has just finished on his latest script, the two-part thriller *Burn Up,* which is based around the politics of oil depletion and climate change. It premiered on BBC2 in June 2008, and starred Neve Campbell, Rupert Penry-Jones, and Bradley Whitford. After adapting *Q&A* into *Slumdog Millionaire,* Simon is now adapting the novel *The Raw Shark Texts* for Film4.

**DANNY BOYLE (Director)**

Danny Boyle's first feature, *Shallow Grave,* earned him the Alexander Korda Award for Outstanding British Film at the BAFTA Awards, as well as a host of other accolades, including Best Director at the San Sebastian Film Festival, The Empire Award for Best Director and Best British Film, and the London Critics' Circle Film Award for Best British Newcomer. Boyle's second feature, *Trainspotting,* is one of the highest-grossing British films of all time. The critically acclaimed film won four Empire Awards, including Best Director and Best Film, and was nominated for a BAFTA Alexander Korda Award.

In 2002 Boyle made the smash-hit horror film *28 Days Later,* which earned more than $80 million worldwide. The film earned Boyle a Saturn Award for Best Horror Film from the Academy of Science Fiction, Fantasy, and Horror Films.

Boyle's other feature films include *Millions,* starring James Nesbit, Alex Etel, and Lewis McGibbon; *The Beach,* starring Leonardo DiCaprio; *A Life Less Ordinary,* starring Ewan McGregor and Cameron Diaz; *Alien Love Triangle;* and *Sunshine,* starring Cillian Murphy. *Slumdog Millionaire* is his eighth international theatrically released film and won the People's Choice Award at the 2008 Toronto International Film Festival. His work in television includes producing Alan Clark's controversial *Elephant,* and directing *Strumpet, Vacuuming Completely Nude in Paradise,* and the series *Mr. Wroe's Virgins,* for which he received a BAFTA nomination. Boyle's career started in the theatre with Howard Barker's *Victory,* Howard Brenton's *The Genius,* and Edward Bond's *Saved,* which won the Time Out Award. Boyle has also directed five productions for the Royal Shakespeare Company.